DISCARD

# Damn Delicious
## MEAL PREP

FARRO BIBIMBAP
BOWLS (page 243)

# *Damn Delicious* MEAL PREP

## 115 EASY RECIPES FOR LOW-CALORIE, HIGH-ENERGY LIVING

### CHUNGAH RHEE

GRAND CENTRAL
PUBLISHING

New York   Boston

Grand Central Publishing
Hachette Book Group
1290 Avenue of the Americas, New York, NY 10104
grandcentralpublishing.com
twitter.com/grandcentralpub

First Edition: February 2019

Grand Central Publishing is a division of Hachette Book Group, Inc. The Grand Central Publishing name and logo is a trademark of Hachette Book Group, Inc.

The publisher is not responsible for websites (or their content) that are not owned by the publisher.

The Hachette Speakers Bureau provides a wide range of authors for speaking events. To find out more, go to www.hachettespeakersbureau.com or call (866) 376-6591.

Nutritional information for recipes provided by Pam Gibson.

Library of Congress Control Number: 2018958460

ISBNs: 978-1-5387-2942-7 (hardcover); 978-1-5387-2940-3 (ebook)

Printed in the United States of America

LSC-W

10  9  8  7  6  5  4  3  2

To Ben and Butters—
my two favorites in the entire world.

# Contents

# Introduction

This cookbook started as a question: "Could I live to eat *and* eat to live well?"

Two years ago, I was 30 pounds overweight. I was exhausted—burned out, really. I was working too much, eating too much, stressing too much. I was *every-thing* too much. I had a booming and successful food blog that I was proud of, and I was cooking new recipes and posting five times per week. Every single day, I was surrounded by food, and I was surrounded by work, and I didn't know how to balance either of them.

I grew up in a traditional Korean household, where hard work is king. My parents immigrated to the U.S. before I was born, and like any other first-gen American kid, I grew up totally in love with all things American. The more all-American something was, the more I wanted it. (Yes, even if it was actually worse than the Korean version!) My mom would cook amazing Korean food every day, but I'd get most excited when she'd surprise us with her version of baked ziti. She'd use rotini noodles, jarred spaghetti sauce, and a big ball of mozzarella that she'd slice into rounds to top the pasta. I remember watching her gently sawing through the soft cheese, eyes at countertop height, hoping desperately that she'd shred off a little piece to give to me.

Food was always a big deal in our house, and we had no boundaries with it at all. One night we'd have *samgyetang,* and the next we'd pick up cheese-burgers and "Animal Style" fries from In-N-Out. But even though food was a big deal to us, there was something even more important: hard work. From an early age, my parents made it clear to me that I would be going to medical school as soon as I graduated from college, and so, after high school, I duti-fully enrolled at UCLA and started my pre-med classes. Every night, I'd come home exhausted from class and bake something, *anything,* to de-stress from the day. I was totally that person who wouldn't eat until they'd photographed the food and sent it around to everyone they knew. (And back then, that was definitely not a full-time job!)

Eventually, the nagging feeling that I didn't like medicine won out, and I realized I just couldn't go through with it. So I looked for something that would still lead to a secure job and that wouldn't disappoint my parents too much: that's how I ended up with a master's in public health.

Around that time a friend (who was most definitely tired of my endless food photo texts) suggested I start a blog to document what I was cooking. I didn't really have the time with my busy class schedule, but I figured if I worked just a little bit harder during the day, I could make some time at night to post a new recipe. I posted my first recipe in 2011, and today, *Damn Delicious* is a $1.5 million business.

I know that sounds shiny and easy, but in this book, I want to get real—really really—and show my readers that behind every successful American Dream is a story of hard work and sacrifice. And I won't lie, it was *hard*. "Food blogging" isn't exactly an acceptable profession to your typical Korean mom. My parents thought I was nuts and that I was throwing away an opportunity to have "a real job" in public health. On top of that, I was working 80-hour weeks building the blog, usually working alone late into the night on weekends and holidays when everyone else was out having fun.

But I had really achieved the American Dream—I was a successful entrepreneur; I was passionate about my work; I set my own hours and worked for myself; I bought my first home in 2016; and I began traveling as much as I could. Yet, along the way, I'd also achieved something else: the American physique.

I was overweight, often sick, always exhausted, and worst of all, despairing that I could ever get control of my eating habits.

As the site grew, I hired my first employee, then another and another, and I finally felt like I was getting back some of my time and mental energy for my health. But after a grueling day of work, I was so wiped out and so set in bad habits that I didn't know what to do but order takeout. Or I would just graze all day until I had no idea what I'd eaten and why.

But I wanted *desperately* to change my eating habits. Which, let me tell you, is not easy when you're surrounded by "damn delicious" food all day. It's literally *my job* to cook and eat all day. I knew I needed a game plan that would set me up for success, but I had zero ideas as to where to start. So what was really the best way to get me back on track?

Easy. Meal prep.

MASON JAR CHINESE
CHICKEN SALAD (page 102)

# PART I

# Welcome to
# MEAL PREP

# 1

## *What Is* MEAL PREP?

Meal prep is the secret weapon of all those effortlessly fit celebrities who roam around LA—it's what many of the top private chefs do to keep their clients on track and happy.

Meal prep makes it easy to have a perfectly portioned, low-calorie, whole food meal at your fingertips anytime. By meal prepping on the weekends and dividing meals into just-right, calorie-controlled portions, it's just as easy to grab your prepped Korean bibimbap bowl on a busy weeknight as it is to grab a store-bought, sodium-laden version or a take-out, high-calorie version.

That right there—having healthy and delicious food at my fingertips all week, with all the ease of convenience food yet none of the bad stuff—is what got me completely and hopelessly hooked on meal prep.

Finally, eating right for me wasn't just about saying no to the unhealthy stuff—it was about saying yes to the just-as-delicious alternative that was already prepped and waiting for me. And personally, after a long day of exerting every ounce of my willpower at work—developing, testing, writing, and photographing new recipes—plus making time for family and friends, the last thing I have is more willpower for saying no to temptingly unhealthy food. Left to my own devices, it's pizza, please—every time.

I fell for meal prep even harder when I realized how much fun the prepping sessions could be. (Yes, prep work can be fun!) I picked a Sunday to try it out, and I invited a bunch of my friends and family over to prep and cook together for the week. With just an afternoon of cooking together, laughing, hanging out, and drinking way too many mimosas, we had an entire week's worth of healthy, fresh food, all neatly packaged up like a private chef had just walked out. It was so much fun, it didn't even feel like work! I felt like I had barely done any work, yet I'd never been more prepared to rock out a week of healthy eating and good choices. Now our small group of friends and family gets together nearly every Sunday to do meal prep together.

## Myths of Meal Prep

Let me start by saying that this is *not* a weight-loss book. I wrote this book for those who want to achieve and maintain a healthy lifestyle. Doing this should not be a miserable process. I mean, there are burrito bowls and pumpkin donuts involved here!

Meal prep has become increasingly popular in today's health-conscious and schedule-heavy climate. But meal prep doesn't require having all your meals prepared in their entirety. It can simply mean chopping, sorting, or pre-cooking ingredients ahead of time to make your life a little bit easier on hectic weeknights. It is an amazing way to plan ahead, save time, implement portion control, and feed not just one person but the whole family all week! Who doesn't want that?

I also want to say that you don't have to be a fitness fanatic or a bodybuilder to do meal prep. And it doesn't have to always be super healthy with overly dry chicken and withered broccoli.

The purpose of this cookbook is to reinvent meal prep, or at the very least, revitalize what you think of it. Working one-on-one with a nutritionist, I wrote this book to inspire your creativity and show you how many different ways you can actually meal prep with the right kinds of foods.

## Why Meal Prep Will Change Your Life

There are many ways in which meal prep can change your life. Since being introduced to it, I have more free time for other things in life, like taking Butters on a walk so he can troll for poo.

No, but really, I have a better, more wholesome, balanced diet. I eat more regularly, which my body and brain thrive on. I even, unintentionally, dropped a dress size.

A lot of people have the misconception that the purpose of meal prep is purely for dieting, and dieting then leads to thoughts of being hungry and solely eating a lettuce leaf.

Let me tell you that I have been eating all kinds of meals from this very book and I promise you, the variety and moderation are very welcomed by my body. Not to mention, it is so much fun to have an afternoon prepping all your boxes of food for the entire week with your friends and family.

You can also choose your level of involvement. Some people can't stand eating the same meals day after day—and that's totally fine. Even meal prepping half or some of your meals will save you time and the headache of trying to plan out seven different lunches or dinners for the week. The recipes also offer a lot of options for swapping out ingredients. Eating oatmeal for breakfast all week becomes much more palatable when it can be loaded with different toppings!

With meal prep, you can tailor your meals to your nutritional preferences, whether it be caloric intake or dietary restrictions. But when it comes to calories, it is important to stress that you need to consume the right kind of calories—the "healthy" calories. So when someone says that they are limiting their calories because they are on a diet, and the diet consists of cubes of cheese or chocolate pudding, that is not a healthy way to live. This will inevitably lead to major weight gain. It is important to fill yourself with healthy, living, colorful foods! Basically, the full spectrum of the rainbow. Eat plenty of colorful fruits and vegetables and whole grains, and limit refined carbohydrates, sugars, and processed foods.

On average, a female needs about 2,000 calories a day to maintain her current weight and about 1,500 calories to lose 1 pound per week. An average man needs about 2,500 calories a day to maintain his current weight and 2,000 calories to lose 1 pound of weight per week. These numbers can vary due to many factors like weight, size, height, activity level, illness, disease, or lifestyle choices. For example, a female athlete may need closer to 2,500 to 3,000 calories to maintain her current weight and muscle.

I hope that sheds some light on meal prep and why I love it. I know you will too! I can't wait to hear and see all of your own meal prep journeys as you work your way through this cookbook!

# 2
## *How to Prep for*
# MEAL PREP

## Meal Prep Containers

I personally love my **glass containers** as they are much easier to clean, but the downside is that they are very heavy. It makes it difficult to carry them around all day, but if you work from home, I would definitely push for glass containers.

**Plastic containers,** on the other hand, are so much lighter, BPA-free, and dishwasher-safe. They also come in different shapes and have compartments for sectioning foods for you type A peeps out there (don't worry, I am VERY type A). They are also easy to stack, which saves on storage space in your cabinets.

You can find meal prep containers on Amazon.com with tons of varieties to choose from. Just be sure to order them three to four days in advance so you don't run out of containers before your next meal prep week!

Another meal prep container that is very useful is the **mason jar.** Inexpensive and amazingly versatile, the jars help with portion control and are portable, BPA-free, and microwave-, fridge-, and oven-safe—and even freezer-safe for some varieties. They also come in different sizes for different purposes.

## Tips for Cooking in Bulk

- **DON'T BE OVERWHELMED.** Dedicating a few hours during the weekend to cooking in bulk will save you much time, stress, and mental burden in the week ahead. Promise!

- **PLANNING AHEAD IS KEY.** Take some time to plan out what you're going to make, create a grocery list, and buy all your ingredients in one trip to avoid any emergency grocery runs. I've also created a handy planning sheet and blank grocery list that you can fill out and take with you! They're in the back of the book (or you can download them at damndelicious.net).

- **BULK STORES ARE YOUR SAVIOR.** When it comes to bulk cooking, Costco is my number 1 stop for large quantities of quality meat, veggies, and fruit. If you don't have a membership, call up your coworker/friend/neighbor/ distant relative who does, make it a joint trip, and meal prep together!

- **USE HELP.** There's no shame in that at all. Shortcuts exist for a reason! So instead of dicing and chopping 10,000 pounds of vegetables and garlic with those sticky fingers, your food processor will come in very handy here. If you don't have a food processor, use the next best thing. Your husband.

- **AL DENTE IS NOT JUST FOR PASTA.** Vegetables should be slightly under-cooked so that they can stay firm when frozen and reheated (without running the risk of being overcooked during the second round of cooking).

- **YOUR FREEZER IS YOUR BEST FRIEND.** Put your freezer to work so you can whip up dinner in a pinch by simply reheating your favorite White Chicken Chili (page 237) with a warm Flaky Mile-High Whole Wheat Biscuit (page 205). Just be sure to freeze in individual, usable portions. It will make your life so much easier.

- **LET COOL COMPLETELY.** You always see this in recipes but really, to keep food safe, cool your foods before freezing them.

- **NOBODY LIKES AIR BUBBLES.** When using ziplock freezer bags, it's all about the seal, so squeeze out all the excess air as best as you can to prevent freezer burn and dehydration.

- **DON'T FORGET TO LABEL ALL YOUR FREEZER BAGS.** Use a permanent marker to label each container with the name of the recipe, the date, and any instructions for thawing/reheating.

## What You'll Need for Big-Batch Cooking

- Large stockpot or Dutch oven
- Casserole dish
- Baking sheets
- Hand mixer
- Immersion blender (a Vitamix or high-speed blender will also work)
- Slow cooker
- Storage freezer bags
- Meal prep containers
- Mason jars
- Food processor
- Other bonus things that may be helpful: time and patience, friends to cook with, the Spice Girls' "Wannabe" to dance to, and/or *This Is Us* to watch if you feel like you need a good cry while cooking and prepping.

## How to Freeze and Store Soups

Leftover soup will typically last two to three days in the refrigerator but it will last at least a month in the freezer.

Be sure to let the soup cool completely prior to freezing. Portion the soup into ziplock freezer bags in individual servings, squeezing out any excess air before sealing. Lay the bags flat in a single layer in the freezer (this will help them freeze quickly). You can stack them once they are frozen to save on storage space. To reheat, thaw overnight in the fridge, then warm over low heat, stirring occasionally, until heated through.

Soups with pasta or dairy do not hold up well in the freezer. But fret no more—simply hold back on the pasta and/or dairy and freeze without it. You can simply add it in upon reheating.

# 3
# MEAL PREP
## *Menus*

Nothing is worse than buying a bunch of veggies, only to throw half of them out when they go bad. If you're looking for a way to ease into meal prep, these four themed meal prep menus and shopping lists are a great way to get you started. By planning ahead and choosing recipes that share similar themes, you can save money and use up all your ingredients! As you get more comfortable meal prepping, you can add more meal choices and variety to your rotation.

# Option 1. *Theme: Kale*

## MENU

| | | |
|---|---|---|
| **BREAKFAST** | Sweet Potato–Kale Hash (page 48) | 287 CALORIES |
| **LUNCH** | Very Green Mason Jar Salad (page 123) | 250 CALORIES |
| **SNACK** | Kale Chips Snack Box (page 175) | 308 CALORIES |
| **DINNER** | White Beans with Sausage and Stir-Fried Kale (page 269) | 392 CALORIES |
| **DRINK** | Green Protein Smoothie (page 72) | 194 CALORIES |

## SHOPPING LIST

**PRODUCE**

3 cups baby spinach
6 bunches kale
1 pound small zucchini
½ cup pea shoots
1 English cucumber
3 medium sweet potatoes
6 cloves garlic
1 onion
½ avocado
2 green onions
1 cup fresh basil
1 tablespoon fresh rosemary
2 tablespoons fresh cilantro
2 handfuls fresh parsley
1 cup grapes
4 tangerines
2 fresh limes
1 banana
1 pint strawberries
½ cup blueberries
1 cup blackberries

**FROZEN**

1 cup green peas

**DAIRY/MEAT**

4 large eggs
¾ cup unsweetened almond milk
½ cup reduced-fat feta cheese
¾ cup 2% Greek yogurt
1 package (12.8 ounces) smoked Andouille sausage
8 ounces turkey breakfast sausage

**PANTRY**

¾ cup pearled barley
2 cans (15.5 ounces each) cannellini beans
1 can (16 ounces) garbanzo beans
1½ cups low-sodium chicken broth
8 tablespoons vanilla protein powder

**STAPLES**

Olive oil
Chili lime seasoning
Crushed red pepper flakes
Dried rosemary
Dried thyme
Dried oregano
Kosher salt
Black pepper

# Option 2. Theme: Rainbow Veggies

## MENU

| | | |
|---|---|---|
| **BREAKFAST** | Crustless Mini Egg Muffins (page 40) | 34 CALORIES |
| **LUNCH** | Thai Chicken Buddha Bowls (page 113) | 503 CALORIES |
| **SNACK** | Rainbow Hummus Veggie Pinwheels (page 179) | 320 CALORIES |
| **DINNER** | Whole Wheat Pad Thai Bowls (page 276) | 439 CALORIES |
| **DRINK** | Carrot Ginger Smoothie (page 64) | 195 CALORIES |

## SHOPPING LIST

**PRODUCE**

¼ cup baby spinach
1 zucchini
1 red cabbage
1 purple cabbage
1 bunch kale
3 red bell peppers
1 yellow bell pepper
4 radishes
1 cup bean sprouts
4 carrots
¼ cup thinly sliced cucumbers
¼ cup alfalfa sprouts
2 green onions
1 shallot
1 tablespoon freshly grated ginger
5 cloves garlic
1 red chile pepper
1 bunch fresh cilantro
2 tablespoons chopped fresh dill
½ cup strawberries
½ cup blueberries
2 navel oranges
4 limes

**DAIRY/MEAT/REFRIGERATED**

2 cups egg whites
2 large eggs
¼ cup crumbled feta
1 cup vanilla Greek yogurt
1 pound boneless, skinless chicken breast
2 tablespoons hummus
1 cup carrot juice

**FROZEN**

2 cups sliced carrots
1½ cups diced pineapple

**PANTRY**

12 ounces whole wheat spaghetti
1 cup farro
3 tablespoons creamy peanut butter

½ cup roasted peanuts
¼ cup chicken stock
1 (8-inch) spinach tortilla
2 tablespoons sambal oelek
3 tablespoons fish sauce

**STAPLES**

Olive oil
Canola oil
Honey
¼ cup reduced-sodium soy sauce
Cornstarch
Dark brown sugar
Light brown sugar
Kosher salt
Black pepper

RAINBOW HUMMUS VEGGIE
PINWHEELS (page 179)

# Option 3. *Theme: Mexican*

## MENU

| | | |
|---|---|---|
| BREAKFAST | Ham, Egg, and Cheese Breakfast Quesadillas (page 39) | 291 CALORIES |
| LUNCH | Chicken Burrito Bowls (page 128) | 488 CALORIES |
| SNACK | Salsa Snack Box (page 180) | 262 CALORIES |
| DINNER | White Chicken Chili (page 237) | 316 CALORIES |
| DRINK | Rainbow Coconut Smoothie (page 79) | 184 CALORIES |

## SHOPPING LIST

**PRODUCE**

2 cups baby spinach
1 orange bell pepper
1 red bell pepper
1 jicama
1 cup chopped broccoli florets
1 small onion
2 tablespoons diced red onion
2 green onions
5 cloves garlic
1 jalapeño chile
2 Anaheim green chile peppers
5 tablespoons chopped fresh cilantro leaves
1 cup blackberries
1 pint blueberries
1 pint strawberries
½ cup raspberries
1 cup diced pineapple
1 pineapple
1 kiwi
2 mangoes
6 tangerines
3 limes

**DAIRY/MEAT/REFRIGERATED**

4 large eggs
½ cup nonfat Greek yogurt
½ cup shredded reduced-fat cheddar cheese
1 cup diced ham
1 pound boneless, skinless chicken breasts
1 pound ground chicken
½ cup pico de gallo

**FROZEN**

1¾ cups corn kernels

**PANTRY**

⅔ cup brown rice
2 cans (15 ounces each) great northern beans
1 can (15 ounces) black beans
4 cups chicken stock
1 chipotle pepper in adobo sauce
2 cups tortilla chips
½ cup flaked coconut
4 (4-inch) whole wheat tortillas
2 cups coconut water

**STAPLES**

Olive oil (regular and extra-virgin)
Honey
Garlic powder
Dried oregano
Paprika
Chili powder
Ground cumin
Onion powder

# Option 4. *Theme: Asian*

## MENU

| | | |
|---|---|---|
| **BREAKFAST** | Tropical Coconut Chia Pudding (page 31) | **432 CALORIES** |
| **LUNCH** | Mason Jar Chinese Chicken Salad (page 102) | **375 CALORIES** |
| **SNACK** | Miso Ginger Detox Soup (page 149) | **97 CALORIES** |
| **DINNER** | Sheet Pan Miso Salmon Dinner (page 255) | **253 CALORIES** |
| **DRINK** | Immune-Boosting Carrot Turmeric Smoothie (page 75) | **89 CALORIES** |

## SHOPPING LIST

**PRODUCE**

3 to 4 bunches kale
1 purple cabbage
1 English cucumber
1 red bell pepper
8 baby bok choy
2 carrots
1 package (3.5 ounces) shiitake mushrooms
1 large piece fresh ginger
5 cloves garlic
10 green onions
1 medium green apple
1 banana
2 mangoes
1 cup diced pineapple

**DAIRY/MEAT/FISH/ REFRIGERATED**

1½ cups 2% Greek yogurt
1 can (13.5 ounces) light coconut milk
8 ounces firm tofu, cubed
1½ cups diced rotisserie chicken
4 (6 ounces each) salmon fillets
6 tablespoons white miso paste
1 cup carrot juice

**FROZEN**

1 cup sliced carrots

**PANTRY**

6 cups vegetable stock
2 tablespoons shredded coconut

1 cup wonton strips
1 teaspoon sesame seeds
½ cup chia seeds
1 sheet kombu

**STAPLES**

Canola oil
Toasted sesame oil
½ cup honey
Maple syrup
Sugar
Vanilla extract
Reduced-sodium soy sauce
½ cup rice wine vinegar
Chili garlic sauce
Ground turmeric
Kosher salt
Black pepper

STUFFED SWEET POTATOES—
4 WAYS (page 150)

# The Recipes

FREEZER BREAKFAST
CROSSANT SANDWICH

# 4. Breakfast

# ALL-AMERICAN BREAKFAST

| PREP TIME:<br>20 MINUTES | COOK TIME:<br>30 MINUTES | TOTAL TIME:<br>50 MINUTES | YIELD:<br>4 SERVINGS |
|---|---|---|---|

12 ounces russet potatoes, diced*

3 tablespoons olive oil, divided

2 cloves garlic, minced

½ teaspoon dried thyme

Kosher salt and freshly ground black pepper, to taste

8 large eggs, lightly beaten

¼ cup shredded reduced-fat Mexican cheese blend

4 slices bacon**

12 ounces broccoli florets (2 to 3 cups)

When it comes to meal prep, most people just think about lunch and dinner. But we cannot forget about the most important meal of the day—breakfast!

Breakfast is a critical part of our daily food intake, but how many of us skip it? Mornings are tough, trying to get out the door for work, school, or meetings, so breakfast often gets missed. That's why I made a meal prep that makes it so easy to have a healthy, hearty, full meal that allows you to start your day off just right and rock that 8:30 a.m. meeting.

- Here are the basic components to a classic breakfast: eggs, potatoes, choice of protein, and a side of fruit.
- Eggs are so nutritious. They are a great source of protein and contain vitamins $B_{12}$, E, and D, making them a great way to kick-start your day.
- When you order breakfast, they usually give you a fruit option but instead, I decided to use broccoli because we should sneak in as many veggies as we possibly can. Plus, broccoli is rich in vitamins, minerals, and dietary fiber. You can always add a little side of your favorite fruit if desired!

1. Preheat the oven to 400 degrees F. Lightly oil a baking sheet or coat with nonstick spray.

2. On the prepared baking sheet, toss the potatoes with 1 tablespoon of the olive oil, the garlic, and thyme; season with salt and pepper. Arrange in a single layer. Bake for 25 to 30 minutes, until golden brown and crisp; set aside.

*(continued)*

### NOTES
* Sweet potatoes can be substituted for the russets.

** Sausage links can be substituted for the bacon.

**NUTRITION FACTS:** CALORIES: 407.0 / TOTAL FAT: 28.0 / TRANS FAT: 0.0 / SATURATED FAT: 6.0 / CHOLESTEROL: 385.0 / SODIUM: 510.0 / CARBOHYDRATES: 27.0 / FIBER: 1.0 / SUGAR: 1.0 / PROTEIN: 21.0

3. Heat the remaining 2 tablespoons olive oil in a large skillet over medium-high heat. Add the eggs and whisk until they just begin to set. Season with salt and pepper and continue cooking until thickened and no visible liquid egg remains, 3 to 5 minutes. Top with the cheese, transfer to a bowl, and set aside.

4. Add the bacon to the skillet and cook until brown and crispy, 6 to 8 minutes. Transfer to a paper towel–lined plate.

5. Meanwhile, place the broccoli florets in a steamer or colander set over about an inch of boiling water in a pan. Cover and steam for 5 minutes, or until crisp-tender and vibrant green.

6. Divide the potatoes, eggs, bacon, and broccoli into meal prep containers. Will keep covered in the refrigerator 3 to 4 days. Reheat in the microwave in 30-second intervals until heated through.

# BREAKFAST STUFFED
# SWEET POTATOES

| PREP TIME:<br>10 MINUTES | COOK TIME:<br>60 MINUTES | TOTAL TIME:<br>1 HOUR 10 MINUTES | YIELD:<br>4 SERVINGS |
|---|---|---|---|

2 medium sweet potatoes

1 tablespoon olive oil

2 tablespoons diced red bell pepper

1 garlic clove, minced

$\frac{1}{2}$ teaspoon crushed red pepper flakes

4 cups baby spinach

4 large eggs, lightly beaten

1 teaspoon Italian seasoning

Kosher salt and freshly ground black pepper, to taste

$\frac{1}{2}$ cup shredded reduced-fat cheddar cheese

1 tablespoon chopped fresh chives (optional)

I like to call this my power breakfast. When I know I have a long day ahead of me with an eight-hour shoot or a strenuous workout (say, a double spin class on a Wednesday morning) coming up, this is the breakfast that fuels my body and mind!

Packed with both nutrients and a sweet flavor, sweet potatoes are one of the best foods for you and part of the superfood food group. They are both versatile and healthful, chock-full of disease-preventing, cancer-fighting, and immune-boosting benefits. Not to mention, they taste great! Their natural sugars are slowly released into the bloodstream, helping to ensure a balanced and regular source of energy without the blood sugar spikes that are linked to fatigue and weight gain.

What I really love about this recipe is that you can create any type of egg stuffing for the potatoes. One favorite guilty-pleasure variation is bacon, egg, and cheese. Sometimes I add a small dollop of sour cream on top—but that's only when I know it's legs and butt day at the gym!

1. Preheat the oven to 400 degrees F. Place the potatoes on a baking sheet and bake for 45 minutes to 1 hour, until they are tender and easily pierced with a fork. Let sit until cool enough to handle. Don't turn off the oven.

2. Cut each potato in half horizontally, then carefully scoop out the center of each half, leaving about $\frac{1}{2}$ inch of potato on the skin. Reserve the flesh for another use.*

*(continued)*

**NOTE**
* Scones, muffins, or sweet potato bread would be a great way to repurpose leftover sweet potato.

**NUTRITION FACTS:** CALORIES: 225.0 / TOTAL FAT: 13.0 / TRANS FAT: 0.0 / SATURATED FAT: 5.0 / CHOLESTEROL: 194.0 / SODIUM: 391.0 / CARBOHYDRATES: 16.0 / FIBER: 4.0 / SUGAR: 3.0 / PROTEIN: 12.0

3. Heat the olive oil in a large skillet over medium-high heat. Add the bell pepper and cook, stirring frequently, until tender, 3 to 4 minutes. Stir in the garlic and red pepper flakes, and then the spinach and stir until wilted, 2 to 3 minutes. Add the eggs and Italian seasoning; cook, stirring occasionally with a spatula, until just set, 2 to 3 minutes; season with salt and pepper to taste.

4. Add the egg mixture to the potato skins and sprinkle with the cheese. Place back on the baking sheet and bake in the 400-degree oven for 5 minutes, or until the cheese has melted.

5. Portion into meal prep containers. Will keep covered in the refrigerator 3 to 4 days. Reheat in the microwave in 30-second intervals until heated through. Garnish with chives, if desired, and serve.

# BLUEBERRY OATMEAL YOGURT PANCAKES

| PREP TIME: 5 MINUTES | COOK TIME: 15 MINUTES | TOTAL TIME: 20 MINUTES | YIELD: 4 SERVINGS |
| --- | --- | --- | --- |

½ plus ⅓ cup white whole wheat flour

½ cup old-fashioned rolled oats

1½ teaspoons sugar

½ teaspoon baking powder

½ teaspoon baking soda

¼ teaspoon kosher salt

¾ cup Greek yogurt

½ cup 2% milk

1 teaspoon olive oil

1 large egg

½ cup blueberries

12 strawberries, thinly sliced

2 kiwis, peeled and thinly sliced

¼ cup maple syrup

Call me basic, but I love a good pancake. And back in college, IHOP was a weekend routine. It was endless stacks of pancakes with maple syrup, whipped cream, and chocolate chips. Literally, endless. It was bottomless pancakes for $3.99 or something ridiculous like that.

Nowadays, I am a little wiser, older, and healthier (just a little!). I love re-creating old favorites and trying to develop more-nutrient-packed versions.

Although the recipe is in the breakfast chapter, I actually kind of love these pancakes for dinner, especially after a late-night spin class! So instead of postmating that bossa nova chocolate cake that's literally meant to serve two or three people (which I have actually finished on my own), I'll pop these bad boys right in the microwave for a light, filling dinner that hits every craving!

1. Preheat a nonstick griddle to 350 degrees F or heat a nonstick skillet over medium-high heat. Lightly coat the griddle or skillet with nonstick spray.

2. In a large bowl, combine the flour, oats, sugar, baking powder, baking soda, and salt. In a large glass measuring cup or another bowl, whisk together the yogurt, milk, olive oil, and egg. Pour the wet mixture over the dry ingredients and stir with a rubber spatula just until moist. Add the blueberries and gently toss to combine.

3. Working in batches, scoop ⅓ cup batter for each pancake onto the griddle and cook until bubbles appear on top and the underside is nicely browned, about 2 minutes. Flip and cook the pancakes on the other side, 1 to 2 minutes longer.

4. Divide the pancakes, strawberries, kiwis, and maple syrup into meal prep containers. Will keep covered in the refrigerator 3 to 4 days. To reheat, place in the microwave in 30-second intervals until heated through.

**NUTRITION FACTS:** CALORIES: 337.0 / TOTAL FAT: 12.0 / TRANS FAT: 0.0 / SATURATED FAT: 3.0 / CHOLESTEROL: 13.0 / SODIUM: 222.0 / CARBOHYDRATES: 48.0 / FIBER: 10.0 / SUGAR: 30.0 / PROTEIN: 14.0

# BUDDHA BREAKFAST BOWLS

| PREP TIME: | COOK TIME: | TOTAL TIME: | YIELD: |
|---|---|---|---|
| 10 MINUTES | 40 MINUTES | 50 MINUTES | 4 SERVINGS |

2 cups low-sodium vegetable stock

1 cup brown rice

¼ cup freshly grated Parmesan

1 teaspoon dried thyme

Kosher salt and freshly ground black pepper, to taste

1 cup Brussels sprouts

1 cup cherry tomatoes

8 ounces cremini mushrooms

2 tablespoons olive oil

3 cloves garlic, minced

1 teaspoon Italian seasoning

4 large eggs

2 tablespoons chopped fresh chives (optional)

You know those times when you wake up and think, *What am I going to have for breakfast? Nothing sounds good. Do I want sweet or savory? Ugh, ain't nobody got time for this.* Then you leave the house with a large coffee and a breakfast bar loaded with 15 grams of sugar. Well, that's kind of how this recipe came to life.

Butters woke me up before my alarm, barking at the leaves blowing into the front yard. On this particular morning he barked, he peed, he went back to bed on my side and started snoring. Me? I simply could *not* go back to sleep.

I went to the kitchen to make breakfast but nothing sounded good. As I scanned the fridge for anything and everything, I saw the leftover Chinese take-out container. I opened it up: brown rice—score. I also found one tomato, four eggs, some mushrooms, and Brussels sprouts. Oh, and Parmesan. Because I *never* run out of Parmesan cheese.

When life gives you lemons, make lemonade. Or a bomb-ass breakfast bowl with the most random ingredients on a 4 a.m. wake-up call. Plus, with 12 grams of protein and only 1 gram of sugar, these will keep you filled up all morning long. A huge thank you to Butters and those dangerous leaves!

1. In a large saucepan of vegetable stock, cook the rice according to package instructions. Stir in the Parmesan and thyme and season with salt and pepper to taste.

2. Preheat the oven to 400 degrees F. Lightly oil a baking sheet or coat with nonstick spray.

3. On the prepared baking sheet, combine the Brussels sprouts, tomatoes, and mushrooms with the olive oil, garlic, and Italian seasoning; season with salt and pepper. Gently toss to combine and arrange in a single layer. Bake for 13 to 14 minutes, until the sprouts are tender.

*(continued)*

NUTRITION FACTS: CALORIES: 292.0 / TOTAL FAT: 15.0 / TRANS FAT: 0.0 / SATURATED FAT: 5.0 / CHOLESTEROL: 190.0 / SODIUM: 384.0 / CARBOHYDRATES: 24.0 / FIBER: 3.0 / SUGAR: 1.0 / PROTEIN: 12.0

4. Meanwhile, place the eggs in a small saucepan and cover with cold water by 1 inch. Bring to a boil and cook for 1 minute. Cover the pan with a tight-fitting lid and remove from the heat; let sit for 5 to 6 minutes. Rinse the eggs under cold water for 30 seconds to stop the cooking. Peel and cut in half.

5. Divide the rice into meal prep containers. Top with the Brussels sprouts, tomatoes, mushrooms, and eggs, and garnish with chives, if desired. Will keep covered in the refrigerator 2 to 3 days. Reheat in the microwave in 30-second intervals until heated through.

# MASON JAR CHIA PUDDINGS

| PREP TIME:<br>**15 MINUTES** | COOK TIME:<br>**NONE** | TOTAL TIME:<br>**15 MINUTES** | YIELD:<br>**4 SERVINGS** |
| --- | --- | --- | --- |

Have you ever soaked chia seeds overnight? They turn into the most amazing no-fuss breakfast pudding for your busy mornings. And any one of the three versions below won't bore you through the week, because the puddings can be topped with anything and everything.

And in case you didn't know, chia seeds are considered a superfood. They are also an excellent non-meat protein and are rich in omega-3 fatty acids and antioxidants.

We are using a little bit of sugar in this pudding, but I decreased the amount needed by using honey as well. Honey makes a fantastic sweetener and contains vitamin C, calcium, and iron. Depending on your mood, all three versions will cover all your sweet tooth cravings without giving you a sugar crash mid-morning!

## Creamsicle Chia Pudding

1¼ cups 2% milk

1 cup 2% plain Greek yogurt

½ cup chia seeds

2 tablespoons honey

2 tablespoons sugar

1 tablespoon orange zest

2 teaspoons vanilla extract

Pinch of kosher salt

¾ cup segmented oranges

¾ cup segmented tangerines

½ cup segmented grapefruit

1. In a large bowl, whisk together the milk, Greek yogurt, chia seeds, honey, sugar, orange zest, vanilla, and salt until well combined.

2. Divide mixture evenly into four (16-ounce) mason jars. Refrigerate overnight, or up to 5 days.

3. Serve cold, topped with oranges, tangerines, and grapefruit.

**NUTRITION FACTS:** CALORIES: 315.0 / TOTAL FAT: 12.0 / TRANS FAT: 0.0 / SATURATED FAT: 3.0 / CHOLESTEROL: 13.0 / SODIUM: 222.0 / CARBOHYDRATES: 42.0 / FIBER: 11.0 / SUGAR: 18.0 / PROTEIN: 14.0

TROPICAL
COCONUT CHIA

RAINBOW
LIME CHIA

CREAMSICLE
CHIA

# Rainbow Lime Chia Pudding

1¼ cups 2% milk

1 cup 2% plain Greek yogurt

½ cup chia seeds

2 tablespoons honey

2 tablespoons sugar

2 teaspoons lime zest

2 tablespoons freshly squeezed lime juice

1 teaspoon vanilla extract

Pinch of kosher salt

½ cup chopped strawberries

½ cup diced mango

½ cup diced kiwi

½ cup blueberries

1. In a large bowl, whisk together the milk, yogurt, chia seeds, honey, sugar, lime zest, lime juice, vanilla, and salt until well combined.

2. Divide the mixture evenly into four (16-ounce) mason jars. Cover and refrigerate overnight, or up to 5 days.

3. Serve cold, topped with strawberries, mango, kiwi, and blueberries.

**NUTRITION FACTS:** CALORIES: 337.0 / TOTAL FAT: 12.0 / TRANS FAT: 0.0 / SATURATED FAT: 3.0 / CHOLESTEROL: 13.0 / SODIUM: 222.0 / CARBOHY-DRATES: 48.0 / FIBER: 10.0 / SUGAR: 30.0 / PROTEIN: 14.0

# Tropical Coconut Chia Pudding

1 (13.5-ounce) can lite coconut milk

1 cup 2% plain Greek yogurt

½ cup chia seeds

2 tablespoons honey

2 tablespoons sugar

1 teaspoon vanilla extract

Pinch of kosher salt

1 cup diced mango

1 cup diced pineapple

2 tablespoons shredded coconut

1. In a large bowl, whisk together the coconut milk, yogurt, chia seeds, honey, sugar, vanilla, and salt until well combined.

2. Divide the mixture evenly into four (16-ounce) mason jars. Cover and refrigerate overnight, or up to 5 days.

3. Serve cold, topped with mango and pineapple and sprinkled with coconut.

**NUTRITION FACTS:** CALORIES: 432.0 / TOTAL FAT: 25.0 / TRANS FAT: 0.0 / SATURATED FAT: 14.0 / CHOLESTEROL: 6.0 / SODIUM: 228.0 / CARBOHYDRATES: 47.0 / FIBER: 11.0 / SUGAR: 31.0 / PROTEIN: 15.0

# EASY OVERNIGHT OATS—4 WAYS

| PREP TIME: 10 MINUTES | COOK TIME: NONE | TOTAL TIME: 10 MINUTES | YIELD: 1 SERVING |
|---|---|---|---|

**BASE INGREDIENTS**

½ cup old-fashioned rolled oats

½ cup milk (or non-dairy milk of choice)

**STRAWBERRIES AND CREAM TOPPING**

½ cup strawberries, chopped

¼ cup vanilla yogurt

1 tablespoon mini chocolate chips

**TROPICAL DELIGHT TOPPING**

2 tablespoons diced kiwi

2 tablespoons diced pineapple

¼ cup nonfat Greek yogurt

1 tablespoon toasted coconut flakes

**BLUEBERRY LEMON CHEESECAKE TOPPING**

¼ cup nonfat Greek yogurt

2 tablespoons blueberry yogurt

¼ cup blueberries

1 teaspoon grated lemon zest

1 teaspoon honey

**PUMPKIN PIE TOPPING**

¼ cup nonfat Greek yogurt

2 tablespoons pumpkin puree

2 tablespoons pecans, chopped

1 teaspoon maple syrup

These could not be simpler to prep. Just add oats and milk to a jar and put it in the fridge until ready to eat. That's overnight oats. Literally.

This is also a great recipe to get the kids involved in cooking since they get to choose their own toppings. My friend Kate has four-year-old twin boys, and she said they wake up so excited to see the overnight oat creations they made the night before. Without even realizing it, she put the fun back into breakfast and they start the day with a nutritious meal!

The great thing about oats is their versatility. They are super healthy, packed full of fiber, help lower cholesterol, and can help with weight loss.

As always, you can choose any toppings you want. Or take your pick from the four featured here. Just remember—fresh fruit is always the best way to sweeten your oats. Try to avoid refined sugars. When you can, substitute cacao nibs for chocolate chips, agave or stevia for sugar and honey, or nonfat plain yogurt for vanilla yogurt.

1. Combine the oats and milk in a 16-ounce mason jar; top with desired toppings.

2. Refrigerate overnight or up to 3 days; serve cold.

**NUTRITION FACTS:**

**STRAWBERRIES AND CREAM OATS:** CALORIES: 343.0 / TOTAL FAT: 11.0 / TRANS FAT: 0.0 / SATURATED FAT: 4.0 / CHOLESTEROL: 15.0 / SODIUM: 95.0 / CARBOHYDRATES: 51.0 / FIBER: 5.0 / SUGAR: 6.0 / PROTEIN: 12.0

**TROPICAL DELIGHT OATS:** CALORIES: 345.0 / TOTAL FAT: 10.0 / TRANS FAT: 0.0 / SATURATED FAT: 4.0 / CHOLESTEROL: 20.0 / SODIUM: 90.0 / CARBOHYDRATES: 44.5 / FIBER: 6.0 / SUGAR: 15.0 / PROTEIN: 15.0

**BLUEBERRY LEMON CHEESECAKE OATS:** CALORIES: 365.0 / TOTAL FAT: 12.0 / TRANS FAT: 0.0 / SATURATED FAT: 5.0 / CHOLESTEROL: 23.0 / SODIUM: 93.0 / CARBOHYDRATES: 52.0 / FIBER: 5.0 / SUGAR: 27.0 / PROTEIN: 16.0

**PUMPKIN PIE OATS:** CALORIES: 424.0 / TOTAL FAT: 18.0 / TRANS FAT: 0.0 / SATURATED FAT: 6.0 / CHOLESTEROL: 20.0 / SODIUM: 145.0 / CARBOHYDRATES: 50.0 / FIBER: 4.0 / SUGAR: 15.0 / PROTEIN: 17.0

PUMPKIN PIE

BLUEBERRY LEMON
CHEESECAKE

STRAWBERRIES
AND CREAM

TROPICAL
DELIGHT

# FREEZER BREAKFAST CROISSANT SANDWICHES

| PREP TIME: | COOK TIME: | TOTAL TIME: | YIELD: |
|---|---|---|---|
| 10 MINUTES | 5 MINUTES | 15 MINUTES | 8 SERVINGS |

1 tablespoon olive oil

4 large eggs, lightly beaten

Kosher salt and freshly ground black pepper, to taste

8 mini croissants, halved horizontally

4 ounces thinly sliced ham

4 slices cheddar cheese, halved

As some of my readers know, I was able to travel to one of my dream locations in the summer of 2016—Paris. I even got to take Butters with me! I was so excited to get there, I literally didn't sleep a wink on the plane. Butters, however, snored and drooled on me the entire journey. Rough life, no? My first stop—before I even checked into my hotel—was to a boulangerie to buy my first freshly baked Parisian croissant.

Now I'm sure you are already thinking that croissants aren't the healthiest breakfast items. But that's why I created these 200-calorie mini sandwiches. I've got you guys covered.

To me, these little bad boys are cute reminders of my amazing trip to Paris. I can pretty much taste a little bit of Paris whenever I want! But the best part is that I can make a batch and freeze them so I can have them anytime, anywhere!

1. Heat the olive oil in a large skillet over medium-high heat. Add the eggs and cook, stirring gently with a silicone or heat-proof spatula, until they just begin to set; season with salt and pepper. Continue cooking until thickened and no visible liquid egg remains, 3 to 5 minutes.

2. Fill the croissants with the eggs, ham, and cheese to make 8 sandwiches. Wrap tightly in plastic wrap and freeze for up to 1 month.

3. To reheat, remove the plastic wrap from a frozen sandwich and wrap in a paper towel. Microwave, flipping halfway, for 1 to 2 minutes, until heated through completely.

**NUTRITION FACTS:** CALORIES: 205.0 / TOTAL FAT: 23.5 / TRANS FAT: 0.0 / SATURATED FAT: 9.0 / CHOLESTEROL: 119.0 / SODIUM: 555.0 / CARBOHYDRATES: 29.0 / FIBER: 4.0 / SUGAR: 5.0 / PROTEIN: 21.0

# GARLIC MUSHROOM OATMEAL

| PREP TIME: | COOK TIME: | TOTAL TIME: | YIELD: |
|---|---|---|---|
| 10 MINUTES | 20 MINUTES | 30 MINUTES | 4 SERVINGS |

2 cups old-fashioned rolled oats

Kosher salt and freshly ground black pepper, to taste

1 tablespoon olive oil

4 cloves garlic, minced

¼ cup diced shallots

8 ounces cremini mushrooms, thinly sliced

½ cup frozen peas

1 teaspoon dried thyme

½ teaspoon dried rosemary

2 cups baby spinach

Grated zest of 1 lemon

¼ cup freshly grated Parmesan (optional)

I have a travel bucket list that I made when I was 20; Italy has been on the list for ten years now. It's been a dream destination of mine, and in 2017 I was fortunate to attend the Barilla World Pasta Championship in Parma. The ancient ruins. The pasta. The cheese. The pizza. Again, *the pasta*.

And I came back to LA with this idea: A mushroom risotto, in breakfast form. With oatmeal. I know, I know. You might be thinking, *Ummmmm*, oatmeal?! But trust me. You'll be welcoming this breakfast alternative to your table in seconds.

I added peas because, hey, sneaking in some veggies is never a bad idea, especially for breakfast. You're welcome, guys!

1. Combine the oats, 3½ cups water, and a pinch of salt in a small saucepan over medium heat. Cook, stirring occasionally, until the oats have softened, about 5 minutes.

2. Heat the olive oil in a large skillet over medium-high heat. Add the garlic and shallots and cook, stirring frequently, until fragrant, about 2 minutes. Add the mushrooms, peas, thyme, and rosemary and cook, stirring occasionally, until tender and browned, 5 to 6 minutes; season with salt and pepper. Stir in the spinach until wilted, about 2 minutes.

3. Stir the oats and lemon zest into the vegetables until well combined. Divide the mixture into meal prep containers and garnish with Parmesan, if desired. Refrigerate for up to 3 days.

4. To serve, stir in up to ¼ cup water, 1 tablespoon at a time, until desired consistency is reached. The oatmeal can then be reheated in the microwave in 30-second intervals until heated through.

**NUTRITION FACTS:** CALORIES: 322.0 / TOTAL FAT: 14.0 / TRANS FAT: 0.0 / SATURATED FAT: 4.0 / CHOLESTEROL: 190.0 / SODIUM: 456.0 / CARBOHYDRATES: 35.0 / FIBER: 5.0 / SUGAR: 2.0 / PROTEIN: 15.0

# HAM, EGG, AND CHEESE BREAKFAST QUESADILLAS

| PREP TIME:<br>10 MINUTES | COOK TIME:<br>20 MINUTES | TOTAL TIME:<br>30 MINUTES | YIELD:<br>4 SERVINGS |
| --- | --- | --- | --- |

1 tablespoon olive oil

2 cloves garlic, minced

1 cup diced ham

1 cup chopped broccoli florets

4 large eggs, lightly beaten

Kosher salt and freshly ground black pepper, to taste

2 green onions, thinly sliced

4 (4-inch) whole wheat tortillas

½ cup shredded reduced-fat cheddar cheese

½ cup raspberries

½ cup blueberries

4 tangerines, peeled and segmented

I know, I'm kind of a genius here: I added broccoli to sneak those vital greens and nutrients into your breakfast. But don't worry. I promise that you'll barely taste the broccoli among all the other fun flavors packed into these quesadillas.

The balance in these boxes is perfect: You have your healthy carbs, protein, vitamins, and minerals all under one roof.

But feel free to change up what you put in your quesadillas. You can use egg whites as opposed to whole eggs; asparagus, spinach, or kale instead of broccoli; and any kind of fruit you want on the side. And, if you're anything like me and you carry some hot sauce in your purse, a little bit of Tabasco will do wonders for your quesadilla. Just saying!

1. Preheat the oven to 400 degrees F. Line a baking sheet with parchment paper.

2. Heat the olive oil in a large skillet over medium-high heat. Add the garlic and cook, stirring frequently, until fragrant, about 1 minute. Stir in the ham and broccoli, and cook until the broccoli is tender and bright green, 3 to 4 minutes.

3. Add the eggs to the skillet and cook, stirring gently with a silicone or heatproof spatula, until they just begin to set; season with salt and pepper. Continue cooking until thickened and no visible liquid egg remains, 3 to 5 minutes. Stir in the green onions.

4. Layer half of each tortilla with the egg mixture; sprinkle with the cheese. Fold in half and place on the prepared baking sheet. Bake until the cheese has melted, 5 to 6 minutes.

5. Place the quesadillas, raspberries, blueberries, and tangerine segments into meal prep containers. Will keep covered in the refrigerator 3 to 4 days. The quesadillas can be reheated in the microwave in 30-second intervals until heated through.

**NUTRITION FACTS:** CALORIES: 291.0 / TOTAL FAT: 12.0 / TRANS FAT: 0.0 / SATURATED FAT: 3.0 / CHOLESTEROL: 204.0 / SODIUM: 802.0 / CARBOHYDRATES: 24.0 / FIBER: 3.0 / SUGAR: 11.0 / PROTEIN: 20.0

# CRUSTLESS MINI EGG MUFFINS

| PREP TIME:<br>10 MINUTES | COOK TIME:<br>25 MINUTES | TOTAL TIME:<br>35 MINUTES | YIELD:<br>MAKES 12 MINI MUFFINS (1 PER SERVING) |
|---|---|---|---|

⅔ cup shredded zucchini

⅔ cup diced red bell pepper

¼ cup crumbled feta cheese

2 tablespoons chopped fresh dill

2 cups egg whites*

Kosher salt and freshly ground black pepper, to taste

My recipes don't just happen overnight. Some take trial and many, many errors. After some frustration, and making and consuming 12 mini egg muffins, I finally nailed this one down: You have just enough veggies, herbs, and cheese to keep these bad boys light and filling. And remember, you don't need much salt, if any, because the feta provides just the right amount.

You can use whole eggs instead of the whites (you'll need about 10 medium eggs to get 2 cups). Yolks are not bad for you at all—they actually contain the majority of an egg's nutrients! I just prefer egg whites sometimes as they keep the calorie count lower for those of us watching our intake.

1. Preheat the oven to 350 degrees F. Lightly coat the cups of a 12-cup mini muffin tin with nonstick spray.

2. Spoon the zucchini, bell pepper, feta, and dill in even layers into the prepared cups. Top with the egg whites until three-fourths full; season with salt and pepper.

3. Bake for 20 to 25 minutes, until just set in the center. Let cool.

4. Store in a ziplock bag or meal prep container in the refrigerator for up to 3 days. To reheat, microwave at 20-second intervals until heated through.

NOTE
* Egg whites in cartons can be found near the eggs at most grocery stores. If getting your egg whites from whole eggs, you'll need about 16 medium eggs to get 2 cups of whites.

**NUTRITION FACTS:** CALORIES: 34.0 / TOTAL FAT: 0.0 / TRANS FAT: 0.0 / SATURATED FAT: 0.0 / CHOLESTEROL: 3.0 / SODIUM: 267.0 / CARBOHYDRATES: 0.0 / FIBER: 2.0 / SUGAR: 0.0 / PROTEIN: 6.0

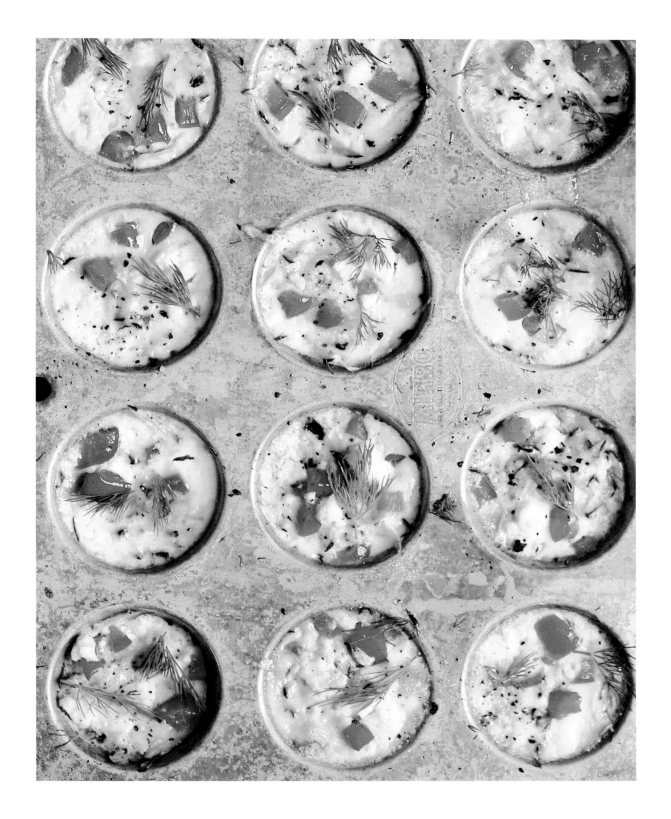

# PB-OATMEAL BREAKFAST BOWL

| PREP TIME:<br>**10 MINUTES** | COOK TIME:<br>**5 MINUTES** | TOTAL TIME:<br>**15 MINUTES** | YIELD:<br>**1 SERVING** |
| --- | --- | --- | --- |

½ cup old-fashioned rolled oats

Pinch of kosher salt

2 tablespoons raspberries

2 tablespoons blueberries

1 tablespoon chopped almonds

½ teaspoon chia seeds

1 banana, thinly sliced*

2 teaspoons peanut butter, warmed**

The best part about this nutritious bowl? No, it's not the peanut butter drizzle. Although that is a close second. It's that it keeps for up to four days in the fridge!

As with most of my recipes, you can substitute ingredients as you like. Instead of peanut butter, you could use almond or cashew butter; apple, mango, pineapple, grapes, raisins, coconut flakes, chocolate chips, or cacao nibs are alternative toppings, among so many more.

But back to that peanut butter drizzle. If you're like me and you *love* peanut butter, then drizzle half of the peanut butter on the bottom of your container *before* adding the cooked oats. It's the best surprise when you hit the bottom of the serving! I always forget I did it until I taste it. It's basically pure oat heaven.

1. Combine 1 cup water, the oats, and salt in a small saucepan. Cook over medium heat, stirring occasionally, until the oats have softened, about 5 minutes.

2. Add the oatmeal to a meal prep container. Top with the raspberries, blueberries, almonds, chia seeds, and banana, and drizzle with the warm peanut butter. Keeps covered in the refrigerator for 3 to 4 days.

3. The oatmeal can be served cold or reheated. Reheat in the microwave at 30-second intervals until heated through.

**NOTES**
\* Add the sliced banana to the bowl just before serving to keep it from turning brown and mushy.
\*\*Peanut butter can be warmed in 10-second increments in the microwave until it is thin enough to drizzle.

**NUTRITION FACTS:** CALORIES: 396.0 / TOTAL FAT: 15.0 / TRANS FAT: 0.0 / SATURATED FAT: 1.0 / CHOLESTEROL: 0.0 / SODIUM: 197.0 / CARBOHYDRATES: 62.0 / FIBER: 11.0 / SUGAR: 16.0 / PROTEIN: 12.0

# PROTEIN POWER WAFFLES

### RECIPE COURTESY OF NICHOLAS HOUNSLOW

| PREP TIME:<br>10 MINUTES | COOK TIME:<br>30 MINUTES (5 MINUTES PER WAFFLE) | TOTAL TIME:<br>40 MINUTES | YIELD:<br>6 WAFFLES |
| --- | --- | --- | --- |

6 large eggs

2 cups cottage cheese

2 cups old-fashioned rolled oats

½ teaspoon vanilla extract

Pinch of kosher salt

3 cups nonfat plain yogurt

1½ cups raspberries

1½ cups blueberries

These waffles are a fan-favorite from the blog, and they have become a weekly staple for us all at Damn Delicious. We snack on them in between our day-long photo shoots, basically to stop us from reaching for the donut box. Hey, after all, it's only 288 calories per waffle box here!

Now, you can make these sweet or savory—it's up to you! For this particular recipe, I made plain protein waffles—or the "OG waffles," as we call them.

I suggest combining it all in a waffle-berry-yogurt sandwich! It does get a little messy but it's so worth it. And hey, I have Butters on standby to lick the mess up off the floor!

You can use different yogurts like soy, goat milk, or even flavored yogurt. But as always, please be mindful if you are counting calories because most other yogurts have a lot more hidden sugars than the plain varieties.

1. Preheat a waffle iron to medium high. Lightly oil the top and bottom of the iron or coat with nonstick spray.

2. Combine the eggs, cottage cheese, oats, vanilla, and salt in a blender and blend until smooth.

3. Pour a scant ½ cup of the egg mixture into the waffle iron, close gently, and cook until golden brown and crisp, 4 to 5 minutes. Repeat with the remaining batter to make additional waffles.

4. Place the waffles, yogurt, raspberries, and blueberries into meal prep containers. Will keep covered in the refrigerator 4 to 5 days.

5. To reheat a waffle, place in a toaster oven on a low setting until heated through.

**NUTRITION FACTS:** CALORIES: 288.0 / TOTAL FAT: 7.0 / TRANS FAT: 0.0 / SATURATED FAT: 2.0 / CHOLESTEROL: 202.0 / SODIUM: 437.0 / CARBOHYDRATES: 33.0 / FIBER: 5.0 / SUGAR: 19.0 / PROTEIN: 21.0

THE BEST DILL
CREAM CHEESE

# SMOKED SALMON MINI-BAGEL BAR

| PREP TIME:<br>15 MINUTES | COOK TIME:<br>NONE | TOTAL TIME:<br>15 MINUTES | YIELD:<br>4 SERVINGS |
| --- | --- | --- | --- |

¼ cup ⅓-less-fat cream cheese, at room temperature

1 green onion, thinly sliced

1 tablespoon chopped fresh dill

1 teaspoon grated lemon zest

¼ teaspoon garlic powder

4 whole wheat mini bagels

8 ounces smoked salmon

½ cup thinly sliced English cucumber

½ cup thinly sliced red onion

2 plum tomatoes, thinly sliced

4 teaspoons capers, drained and rinsed

1 lemon, cut into wedges (optional)

A personalized portable bagel station just for me? Um, yes, please! I would like one for every day this week. Please and thank you. Just don't mind your seething coworkers when they see this and they're stuck with a black coffee and a protein bar.

No, but really, this is a great breakfast loaded with carbs and protein to help fuel your day. And as always, there are so many ways you can tweak the box to cater to your personal preferences.

- You can use any type of bagel you want: sesame, everything, onion, blueberry, etc.
- If you do not like salmon, try smoked turkey or even sliced chicken.
- Steer clear of flavored cream cheeses like blueberry and strawberry as they have a ton of sugar in them, which would potentially increase this 294-calorie box to twice the calories!

1. In a small bowl, combine the cream cheese, green onion, dill, lemon zest, and garlic powder.

2. Place the cheese mixture, bagels, salmon, cucumber, onion, tomatoes, and capers into meal prep containers and add lemon wedges, if desired. These keep in the refrigerator for up to 2 days.

**NUTRITION FACTS:** CALORIES: 294.0 / TOTAL FAT: 5.0 / TRANS FAT: 0.0 / SATURATED FAT: 2.0 / CHOLESTEROL: 21.0 / SODIUM: 863.0 / CARBOHYDRATES: 40.0 / FIBER: 4.0 / SUGAR: 8.0 / PROTEIN: 19.0

# SWEET POTATO-KALE HASH

| PREP TIME:<br>10 MINUTES | COOK TIME:<br>25 MINUTES | TOTAL TIME:<br>35 MINUTES | YIELD:<br>4 SERVINGS |
|---|---|---|---|

4 large eggs

1 tablespoon olive oil

8 ounces turkey breakfast sausage

3 medium sweet potatoes, diced

½ teaspoon dried rosemary

½ teaspoon dried thyme

½ teaspoon dried oregano

Kosher salt and freshly ground black pepper, to taste

4 cups chopped kale

2 tablespoons chopped fresh cilantro leaves

1 cup strawberries

1 cup blackberries

Typically, we use regular russet potatoes for a traditional hash, but sweet potatoes are a much healthier alternative. Sweet potatoes are an excellent source of vitamin A and a very good source of dietary fiber, vitamin C, manganese, copper, pantothenic acid, potassium, niacin, phosphorus, and vitamins $B_6$, $B_1$, and $B_2$. Not to mention, they have more fiber and a lower glycemic index than regular white potatoes!

I use turkey sausage but you can use regular pork sausage, or lamb, chicken, or even veggie sausage. You can also swap out the kale and use spinach or broccoli. Brussels sprouts also work wonders if they're in season! As for the accompaniments, you can use any fruit of your choice. I'm partial to the antioxidants in blueberries since they keep my skin glowing and healthy!

1. Place the eggs in a large saucepan and cover with cold water by 1 inch. Bring to a boil and cook for 1 minute. Cover the pan with a tight-fitting lid and remove from heat; let sit for 5 to 6 minutes. Drain well and let cool before peeling.

2. Heat the olive oil in a large skillet over medium-high heat. Add the sausage and cook until browned, 3 to 5 minutes, breaking up the sausage as it cooks. Drain the excess fat, reserving 1 tablespoon in the skillet, and set the sausage aside.

3. Add the sweet potato, rosemary, thyme, and oregano to the skillet and season with salt and pepper. Cook, stirring occasionally, until the sweet potato is cooked through and tender, 10 to 12 minutes. Stir in the kale and cilantro and cook until the kale is tender, 3 to 5 minutes.

4. Place the hash, berries, and eggs in to meal prep containers. Will keep covered in the refrigerator 3 to 4 days. To serve, reheat the hash in the microwave at 30-second intervals until heated through.

**NUTRITION FACTS:** CALORIES: 287.0 / TOTAL FAT: 14.5 / TRANS FAT: 0.0 / SATURATED FAT: 3.5 / CHOLESTEROL: 237.0 / SODIUM: 460.0 / CARBOHYDRATES: 24.0 / FIBER: 6.0 / SUGAR: 9.0 / PROTEIN: 16.0

ANTIOXIDANT ACAI
BERRY SMOOTHIE

# 5. Smoothies

# BERRY BEET SMOOTHIE

| PREP TIME: 10 MINUTES | COOK TIME: NONE | TOTAL TIME: 10 MINUTES | YIELD: 4 (8-OUNCE) SERVINGS |
| --- | --- | --- | --- |

### TO PREP

1 (8.8-ounce) package cooked beets*

1 cup frozen strawberries

1 cup frozen raspberries

1 tablespoon chia seeds

### TO SERVE

1 cup unsweetened vanilla almond milk

½ cup 2% Greek yogurt

2 tablespoons honey

1 teaspoon vanilla extract

In an effort to get me to eat beets, my parents used to say they tasted like candy. I would inevitably take a big bite—only to be horrified that it tasted, well, not at all like candy. In fact, beets tasted like dirt.

There was no coming back from that. But as I got older and my taste buds matured, I have grown to still hate beets. The only exception is when it comes to this smoothie. It's weird, I know. Maybe it's the berries. Maybe the blend of strawberries and raspberries counterbalances the dense flavor of the beets with their sweetness.

But as much as I dislike beets, they are so incredible for you. Not only are they full of vitamins, they are known to improve overall health. They are rich in nitrates, which help with blood pressure and lowering your risk of heart disease. They can also improve your stamina and fight inflammation, which makes them perfect for consumption before and after a workout.

All in all, this truly is a beet dish that tastes like candy. Not dirt.

1. Combine the beets, strawberries, raspberries, and chia seeds in a large bowl. Divide among 4 ziplock freezer bags. Freeze for up to a month, until ready to serve.

2. TO MAKE ONE SERVING: Place the contents of one bag in a blender and add ¼ cup almond milk, 2 tablespoons yogurt, 1½ teaspoons honey, and ¼ teaspoon vanilla. Blend until smooth. Serve immediately.

### NOTE
* Be sure to grab plain beets and not a flavored variety.

**NUTRITION FACTS:** CALORIES: 126.0 / TOTAL FAT: 2.0 / TRANS FAT: 0.0 / SATURATED FAT: 0.0 / CHOLESTEROL: 3.0 / SODIUM: 132.0 / CARBOHYDRATES: 21.0 / FIBER: 5.0 / SUGAR: 15.0 / PROTEIN: 3.0

CINNAMON
GARNISH

# BANANA-PEANUT BUTTER "MILKSHAKE"

| PREP TIME:<br>5 MINUTES | COOK TIME:<br>NONE | TOTAL TIME:<br>5 MINUTES | YIELD:<br>5 (8-OUNCE) SERVINGS |
|---|---|---|---|

## TO PREP

3 medium bananas, sliced

⅓ cup peanut butter powder (such as PB2)

⅓ cup vanilla protein powder

3 pitted dates

¼ teaspoon ground cinnamon

## TO SERVE

1 cup unsweetened almond milk

½ cup Greek yogurt

Cinnamon (optional)

It really is true. Peanut butter makes *everything* better. That and wine. And Netflix. And Butters' "turkey legging." BUT! Peanut butter, guys. And this milkshake is no exception.

Peanut butter powder, a lower-fat option, has up to 85 percent fewer calories than regular peanut butter, yet it still has the same amount of protein. So each serving here has 11 grams protein! I also love using chocolate peanut butter powder for that Reese's-peanut-butter-cup taste. If you're prepping this as a post-workout smoothie, you could up the protein by adding an extra scoop of protein powder.

So again, as I said earlier, peanut butter truly makes everything better.

1. Combine the bananas, PB powder, protein powder, dates, and cinnamon in a large bowl. Divide among 5 ziplock freezer bags and freeze for up to a month, until ready to serve.

2. TO MAKE ONE SERVING: Place the contents of one bag in a blender and add a generous 3 tablespoons almond milk, 1½ tablespoons yogurt, and ¼ cup ice. Blend until smooth. Sprinkle with cinnamon, if using, and serve immediately.

**NUTRITION FACTS:** CALORIES: 152.0 / TOTAL FAT: 5.0 / TRANS FAT: 0.0 / SATURATED FAT: 0.0 / CHOLESTEROL: 23.0 / SODIUM: 124.0 / CARBOHYDRATES: 22.0 / FIBER: 3.0 / SUGAR: 13.0 / PROTEIN: 11.0

# ANTIOXIDANT ACAI BERRY SMOOTHIE

| PREP TIME: 10 MINUTES | COOK TIME: NONE | TOTAL TIME: 10 MINUTES | YIELD: 4 (12-OUNCE) SERVINGS |
|---|---|---|---|

## TO PREP

2 (3.88-ounce) packages frozen acai puree, thawed

1 cup frozen raspberries

1 cup frozen blueberries

1 cup frozen blackberries

1 cup frozen strawberries

½ cup pomegranate seeds

## TO SERVE

1½ cups pomegranate juice

What exactly is acai? I kept hearing the word throughout the streets of LA and I had no idea. I just knew that it had to be something healthy.

So upon further research, I found that it comes from the acai berry, and it has all the positive health benefits—antioxidants, fiber, and heart-healthy fats, to name a few.

In short, acai berries are very beneficial to us. So I made a smoothie out of acai puree that is packed full of those antioxidants and contains all of my favorite berries in one!

Now this can be either a great meal substitute or a simple healthy breakfast. On the days that I have an early workday or an eight- to ten-hour shoot ahead of me, this is my number 1 choice for breakfast!

And the best part is that this smoothie (and all the others in this chapter) can be prepped and kept in the freezer for up to a month. All you have to do is open the freezer door, grab one of the bags, and throw the contents in the blender with the appropriate liquid (pomegranate juice here). Boom. Done. No more overpriced $9.99 smoothies!

1. Combine the acai, raspberries, blueberries, blackberries, strawberries, and pomegranate seeds in a large bowl. Divide the mixture among 4 ziplock freezer bags. Freeze for up to a month, until ready to serve.

2. TO MAKE ONE SERVING: Place the contents of one bag in a blender, add a generous ⅓ cup pomegranate juice, and blend until smooth. Serve immediately.

**NUTRITION FACTS:** CALORIES: 223.0 / TOTAL FAT: 3.0 / TRANS FAT: 0.0 / SATURATED FAT: 1.0 / CHOLESTEROL: 0.0 / SODIUM: 27.0 / CARBOHYDRATES: 47.0 / FIBER: 9.0 / SUGAR: 35.0 / PROTEIN: 2.0

# BERRY MELON SMOOTHIE

| PREP TIME: 10 MINUTES | COOK TIME: NONE | TOTAL TIME: 10 MINUTES | YIELD: 4 (12-OUNCE) SERVINGS |
|---|---|---|---|

## TO PREP

4 cups diced frozen watermelon

2 cups diced cantaloupe

1 cup frozen raspberries

1/3 cup packed fresh mint leaves

## TO SERVE

1 cup coconut water

4 tablespoons fresh lime juice

2 tablespoons honey

This is my favorite summer refresher! I mean, really, there's nothing like cold melon, enjoyed poolside, to get everyone in the summer spirit. (You can also add a little tequila or vodka to make a perfect pool party drink...but *sssh,* I didn't tell you that!)

The mint is my favorite touch as it adds a fresh kick and reminds me of one of my favorite drinks, the mojito—but with less sugar!

I use honey to sweeten this smoothie but with all the fresh fruits here, you really don't need much of a sweetener at all! I would say 2 tablespoons max but you can probably get away with even 1 tablespoon!

One of my last ingredients is coconut water, which is super hydrating and packed full of electrolytes and nutrients, making this a perfect drink for a hot day by the pool.

1. Combine the watermelon, cantaloupe, raspberries, and mint in a large bowl. Divide among 4 ziplock freezer bags and freeze for up to a month, until ready to serve.

2. TO MAKE ONE SERVING: Place the contents of one bag in a blender and add 1/4 cup coconut water, 1 tablespoon lime juice, and 1 1/2 teaspoons honey. Blend until smooth. Serve immediately.

**NUTRITION FACTS:** CALORIES: 152.0 / TOTAL FAT: 0.0 / TRANS FAT: 0.0 / SATURATED FAT: 0.0 / CHOLESTEROL: 0.0 / SODIUM: 74.0 / CARBOHYDRATES: 36.0 / FIBER: 5.0 / SUGAR: 30.0 / PROTEIN: 2.0

# BLACK FOREST SMOOTHIE

| PREP TIME: | COOK TIME: | TOTAL TIME: | YIELD: |
|---|---|---|---|
| **10 MINUTES** | **NONE** | **10 MINUTES** | **4 (8-OUNCE) SERVINGS** |

## TO PREP

1 (16-ounce) bag frozen pitted sweet cherries

2 cups baby spinach

2 tablespoons cocoa powder

1 tablespoon chia seeds

## TO SERVE

1 cup unsweetened chocolate almond milk

¾ cup vanilla 2% Greek yogurt

3 teaspoons maple syrup

1 teaspoon vanilla extract

A good friend of mine is always struggling to get her toddlers to eat any food with protein. She said every day is a battle that she rarely wins. Until now, that is.

The Black Forest Smoothie is the answer to every parent's plight. It has all the goodness that kids like, plus the nutrients they need. And it has a subtle sweetness that isn't overpowering or full of sugar.

Spinach makes the body strong, but kids rarely eat it. Actually, the same can be said for adults! So packing this smoothie with spinach provides all the benefits of this super veggie, but hides the taste. It is rich in iron, protein, potassium, and vitamin A, and known for many other health benefits.

The real secret ingredient, though, is the chia seeds, which are considered a superfood. They are chock-full of protein, fiber, omega-3 fats, antioxidants, vitamins, and minerals. Using chia seeds is an easy way to ensure you are getting much-needed protein in your diet!

For anyone craving chocolate, the bit of cocoa powder and the chocolate almond milk give you what you need to fight the craving without all the guilt of eating a chocolate bar!

1. Combine the cherries, spinach, cocoa powder, and chia seeds in a large bowl. Divide among 4 ziplock freezer bags. Freeze for up to a month, until ready to serve.

2. TO MAKE ONE SERVING: Place the contents of one bag in a blender and add ¼ cup almond milk, 3 tablespoons yogurt, ¾ teaspoon maple syrup, and ¼ teaspoon vanilla. Blend until smooth. Serve immediately.

**NUTRITION FACTS:** CALORIES: 169.0 / TOTAL FAT: 2.0 / TRANS FAT: 0.0 / SATURATED FAT: 1.0 / CHOLESTEROL: 2.0 / SODIUM: 73.0 / CARBOHYDRATES: 27.0 / FIBER: 4.0 / SUGAR: 21.0 / PROTEIN: 5.0

GRAHAM
CRACKER
GARNISH

# BLUEBERRY PIE SMOOTHIE

| PREP TIME: 10 MINUTES | COOK TIME: NONE | TOTAL TIME: 10 MINUTES | YIELD: 4 (8-OUNCE) SERVINGS |
|---|---|---|---|

## TO PREP

2 ½ cups frozen blueberries

1 banana, sliced

2 whole cinnamon graham crackers, broken into pieces

1 tablespoon almond butter

## TO SERVE

1 cup unsweetened vanilla almond milk

½ cup 2% Greek yogurt

3 teaspoons honey

Let's face it. Pretty much every day, mid-afternoon, you start craving something sweet. I don't know why this happens, but for me, it feels like my internal clock is screaming, "You have to get an old-fashioned donut immediately. Or else."

Not sure what happens at "or else," but I often find myself with the devil on one shoulder begging me to eat sugar and the angel on the other imploring me not to. So, I found the ultimate compromise. This blueberry pie smoothie kicks that sweet craving to the curb, yet you can still feel good about yourself.

The sweetness of the honey offsets a little bit of the blueberries' tartness. Plus, honey contains vitamins and minerals such as riboflavin and iron. And if you can find local honey, it is a great way to combat seasonal allergies!

I like adding a bit of graham cracker to help thicken the smoothie. I also love topping it off with a little crumbled graham cracker for a light crunch. Plus, it really does taste like a blueberry pie!

1. Combine the blueberries, banana, graham crackers, and almond butter in a large bowl. Divide among 4 ziplock freezer bags. Freeze for up to a month, until ready to serve.

2. TO MAKE ONE SERVING: Place the contents of one bag in a blender and add ¼ cup almond milk, 2 tablespoons yogurt, and ¾ teaspoon honey. Blend until smooth. Serve immediately.

**NUTRITION FACTS:** CALORIES: 204.0 / TOTAL FAT: 5.0 / TRANS FAT: 0.0 / SATURATED FAT: 0.0 / CHOLESTEROL: 3.0 / SODIUM: 92.0 / CARBOHYDRATES: 36.0 / FIBER: 4.0 / SUGAR: 25.0 / PROTEIN: 4.0

# CARROT GINGER SMOOTHIE

| PREP TIME: 10 MINUTES | COOK TIME: NONE | TOTAL TIME: 10 MINUTES | YIELD: 4 (12-OUNCE) SERVINGS |
|---|---|---|---|

**TO PREP**

2 navel oranges, peeled, chopped, and seeds removed

2 cups frozen sliced carrots

1½ cups diced frozen pineapple

1 tablespoon finely chopped peeled fresh ginger

**TO SERVE**

1 cup carrot juice

1 cup vanilla Greek yogurt

3 teaspoons honey

If you are like me, you are always hungry. And you often can't decide what you want to eat: sweet...savory...sweet *and* savory... So it's a good thing that this smoothie covers all of that!

It's one of the more substantial smoothies and will really fill you up. It is also a great way to sneak in those veggies for kids or the reluctant adult in the family. They won't even know there's carrots in here—it's just that good!

On top of all that carrot goodness, this smoothie also has a ton of ginger in it! Ginger contains gingerol, which can treat many forms of nausea and morning sickness, reduce muscle pain and soreness, act as a natural anti-inflammatory, and help lower blood sugar and cholesterol levels.

So maybe this is one of those smoothies where it's okay to have more than one serving!

1. Combine the oranges, carrots, pineapple, and ginger in a large bowl. Divide among 4 ziplock freezer bags. Freeze for up to a month, until ready to serve.

2. TO MAKE ONE SERVING: Place the contents of one bag in a blender and add ¼ cup carrot juice, ¼ cup yogurt, and ¾ teaspoon honey. Blend until smooth. Serve immediately.

**NUTRITION FACTS:** CALORIES: 195.0 / TOTAL FAT: 3.0 / TRANS FAT: 0.0 / SATURATED FAT: 2.0 / CHOLESTEROL: 8.0 / SODIUM: 105.0 / CARBOHYDRATES: 36.0 / FIBER: 2.0 / SUGAR: 26.0 / PROTEIN: 8.0

# CREAMY GREEN GODDESS SMOOTHIE

| PREP TIME: | COOK TIME: | TOTAL TIME: | YIELD: |
|---|---|---|---|
| 5 MINUTES | NONE | 5 MINUTES | 6 (8-OUNCE) SERVINGS |

## TO PREP

1 avocado, halved, pitted, and peeled

2 cups baby spinach

2 cups baby kale

1½ cups diced pineapple

1 cup chopped sugar snap peas

⅓ cup vanilla protein powder

## TO SERVE

1½ cups unsweetened almond milk

Avocados are where it's at right now! With their powerful health benefits and ability to be used in so many ways, it's no wonder this superfood is winning popularity contests. The avocado is chock-full of nutrients including fiber, vitamin K, folate, vitamin C, potassium, and many more.

When you mix avocado with greens, you have a perfect smoothie that will make you feel like you've gotten all your necessary vitamins and minerals in one perfect drink. Feel free to use your favorite protein powder or swap out the pineapple for another fruit.

I love drinking this smoothie mid-afternoon when I need a boost to get me to the end of the day!

1. Combine the avocado, spinach, kale, pineapple, snap peas, and protein powder in a large bowl. Divide among 6 ziplock freezer bags. Freeze for up to a month, until ready to serve.

2. TO MAKE ONE SERVING: Place the contents of one bag in a blender and add ¼ cup almond milk. Blend until smooth. Serve immediately.

**NUTRITION FACTS:** CALORIES: 102.0 / TOTAL FAT: 3.0 / TRANS FAT: 0.0 / SATURATED FAT: 0.0 / CHOLESTEROL: 21.0 / SODIUM: 89.0 / CARBOHYDRATES: 10.0 / FIBER: 1.0 / SUGAR: 6.0 / PROTEIN: 8.0

# GARDEN KIWI SMOOTHIE

| PREP TIME: | COOK TIME: | TOTAL TIME: | YIELD: |
|---|---|---|---|
| 10 MINUTES | NONE | 10 MINUTES | 4 (12-OUNCE) SERVINGS |

### TO PREP

4 kiwis, peeled and sliced

2 cups packed baby spinach

1 cup sliced banana

2 tablespoons chia seeds

### TO SERVE

1 cup vanilla Greek yogurt

1 head Boston lettuce

3 Persian cucumbers, sliced

As I have said before, life isn't always about donuts and coffee... although it really should be. But I will say this: As far as drinking your greens, this smoothie is one of the best ways to consume them. You won't even know they're there because the smoothie tastes so sweet.

I mean, look at how pretty these smoothie ingredients are! I honestly loved shooting this so much, I had the photo printed and placed on my fridge. Every time I look at it, I feel healthier. It also acts as a friendly reminder to eat my greens.

Chia seeds are another secret weapon I like to keep in my arsenal. And no, they aren't just those seeds that get stuck in your teeth. They also have amazing health benefits as they are high in antioxidants, minerals, omega-3s, protein, and dietary fiber. Note: If you want to lower the sugar content, you can use plain natural yogurt instead of vanilla.

1. Combine the kiwi, spinach, banana, and chia seeds in a large bowl. Divide among 4 ziplock freezer bags. Freeze for up to a month, until ready to serve.

2. TO MAKE ONE SERVING: Place the contents of one bag in a blender and add $1/4$ cup yogurt, $1/2$ cup torn lettuce leaves, and sliced cucumber. Blend until smooth. Serve immediately.

**NUTRITION FACTS:** CALORIES: 212.0 / TOTAL FAT: 5.0 / TRANS FAT: 0.0 / SATURATED FAT: 2.0 / CHOLESTEROL: 8.0 / SODIUM: 44.0 / CARBOHYDRATES: 34.0 / FIBER: 7.0 / SUGAR: 18.0 / PROTEIN: 10.0

# GREEN DETOX SMOOTHIE

| PREP TIME: 10 MINUTES | COOK TIME: NONE | TOTAL TIME: 10 MINUTES | YIELD: 4 (8-OUNCE) SERVINGS |
| --- | --- | --- | --- |

**TO PREP**

2 cups baby spinach

2 cups baby kale

2 stalks celery, chopped

1 medium green apple, cored and chopped

1 cup sliced banana

1 tablespoon grated fresh ginger

1 tablespoon chia seeds

**TO SERVE**

1 cup unsweetened almond milk

3 teaspoons honey

Growing up, my mom made a green smoothie similar to this. And you know what? It tasted awful. Just horrible.

She would hand me a glass of the greenest smoothie ever and I would sneak to the bathroom and pour it down the sink. Then I got caught red-handed. For punishment, she made me drink two servings, in their entirety, in front of her.

But this smoothie is nothing like that. It may not be your kid's favorite since it's super green and all, but hey, that's why we have the banana and apples for their added sweetness.

However, it is a bikini-ready smoothie for us grown-ups. It's loaded with plenty of superfoods, plus ginger to heal any tummy issues. You'll feel energized, detoxed, and ready to go every single morning.

And I promise: It won't see your sink's drain.

1. Combine the spinach, kale, celery, apple, banana, ginger, and chia seeds in a large bowl. Divide among 4 ziplock freezer bags. Freeze for up to a month, until ready to serve.

2. TO MAKE ONE SERVING: Place the contents of one bag in a blender and add ¼ cup almond milk and ¾ teaspoon honey. Blend until smooth. Serve immediately.

**NUTRITION FACTS:** CALORIES: 136.0 / TOTAL FAT: 1.0 / TRANS FAT: 0.0 / SATURATED FAT: 0.0 / CHOLESTEROL: 0.0 / SODIUM: 104.0 / CARBOHYDRATES: 28.0 / FIBER: 4.0 / SUGAR: 17.0 / PROTEIN: 1.0

# GREEN PROTEIN SMOOTHIE

| PREP TIME:<br>5 MINUTES | COOK TIME:<br>NONE | TOTAL TIME:<br>5 MINUTES | YIELD:<br>4 (8-OUNCE) SERVINGS |
|---|---|---|---|

## TO PREP

3 cups baby spinach

1 banana, sliced

½ avocado, pitted and peeled

½ cup blueberries

2 handfuls fresh parsley leaves

8 tablespoons vanilla protein powder

## TO SERVE

1 cup sliced cucumber

¾ cup unsweetened almond milk

I call this my *diet smoothie* because it is my go-to when I feel I have overindulged, particularly around the holidays. But honestly, I find that I sleep better after this quick nutrient boost, and I get to give my digestive tract—and jeans—a bit of a break!

One of the most powerful ingredients here is the parsley: It's an excellent source of vitamin K and C, and is also a good source of vitamin A, folate, and iron. It can help boost your immune system, relieve symptoms of arthritis, and act as a general cleanser of the body.

This is, again, one of those smoothies where you can sneak in the greens without it tasting too "healthy." I told you guys I'd take care of you!

You can use any type of protein powder, from whey to vegan. You can also use any kind of milk based on your personal or dietary preference. Almond milk is just what I prefer for this one.

1. Combine the spinach, banana, avocado, blueberries, parsley, and protein powder in a large bowl. Divide among 4 ziplock freezer bags. Freeze for up to a month, until ready to serve.

2. TO MAKE ONE SERVING: Place the contents of one bag in a blender and add ¼ cup cucumber and 3 tablespoons almond milk. Blend until smooth. Serve immediately.

**NUTRITION FACTS:** CALORIES: 194.0 / TOTAL FAT: 3.0 / TRANS FAT: 0.0 / SATURATED FAT: 0.0 / CHOLESTEROL: 40.0 / SODIUM: 178.0 / CARBOHYDRATES: 16.0 / FIBER: 1.0 / SUGAR: 9.0 / PROTEIN: 25.0

# IMMUNE-BOOSTING CARROT TURMERIC SMOOTHIE

| PREP TIME: 5 MINUTES | COOK TIME: NONE | TOTAL TIME: 5 MINUTES | YIELD: 4 (8-OUNCE) SERVINGS |
|---|---|---|---|

## TO PREP

1 cup sliced frozen carrots

1 banana, sliced

1 medium green apple, cored and chopped

1 (1-inch) piece fresh ginger, peeled and sliced

1 teaspoon ground turmeric, or more to taste

## TO SERVE

1 cup carrot juice

½ cup 2% Greek yogurt

4 teaspoons maple syrup

½ teaspoon vanilla extract

Let's face it—getting through the winter months unscathed by illness is no easy feat. Especially if you are a parent or work in an environment with a lot of people. It can feel overwhelming trying to figure out what to do to thwart any oncoming sickness. That's why we have this immune-boosting smoothie, which is full of bacteria-fighting ingredients—plus, it tastes great.

Carrots, as you know from the Carrot Ginger Soup on page 189, are high in vitamin A, which supports a healthy immune system. Bananas are high in potassium, vitamin $B_6$, and antioxidants. Apples are high in fiber, which aids in digestion, and they also contain vitamins C and K.

But turmeric is the true star of this smoothie. It's an herb, native to India, that has been used for medicinal purposes for thousands of years. An important component of turmeric is curcumin, known for its strong anti-inflammatory abilities. Many studies have shown that curcumin can be just as good as some pharmaceutical options for reducing inflammation! Turmeric is also known to soothe the stomach and aid in digestion.

Even if you *aren't* feeling under the weather, this is a great smoothie to begin your day and give you that boost of energy during that dreaded mid-morning slump!

1. Combine the carrots, banana, apple, ginger, and turmeric in a large bowl. Divide among 4 ziplock freezer bags. Freeze for up to a month, until ready to serve.

2. TO MAKE ONE SERVING: Place the contents of one bag in a blender and add ¼ cup carrot juice, 2 tablespoons yogurt, a generous teaspoon maple syrup, ⅛ teaspoon vanilla, and ¼ cup ice. Blend until smooth. Serve immediately.

**NUTRITION FACTS:** CALORIES: 89.0 / TOTAL FAT: 1.0 / TRANS FAT: 0.0 / SATURATED FAT: 0.0 / CHOLESTEROL: 3.0 / SODIUM: 31.0 / CARBOHYDRATES: 19.0 / FIBER: 2.0 / SUGAR: 11.0 / PROTEIN: 3.0

# PEACH MELBA SMOOTHIE

| PREP TIME: 5 MINUTES | COOK TIME: NONE | TOTAL TIME: 5 MINUTES | YIELD: 6 (8-OUNCE) SERVINGS |
|---|---|---|---|

## TO PREP

1 (16-ounce) package frozen sliced peaches

1 cup frozen raspberries

1 orange, peeled and seeded

1/3 cup vanilla protein powder

## TO SERVE

1/2 cup orange juice

2 tablespoons fresh lime juice

3 teaspoons honey

1 1/2 teaspoons vanilla extract

Peaches are one of my favorite fruits. They are low in calories, have zero saturated fat and cholesterol, and contain a great deal of fiber. Peaches also have important minerals we need: calcium, potassium, magnesium, iron, manganese, phosphorus, zinc, and copper. Adding protein powder ensures that you get a nutritionally packed smoothie that is also a great post-workout snack.

Now that I have given you all the healthy info, we can talk about a less-healthy variation: It can be the base for a great summer pool-party drink—just add some rum or vodka for that extra kick! It's just such a great drink to sip while floating around the pool on a hot day.

1. Combine the peaches, raspberries, orange, and protein powder in a large bowl. Divide among 6 ziplock freezer bags. Freeze for up to a month, until ready to serve.

2. TO MAKE ONE SERVING: Place the contents of one bag in a blender and add 4 teaspoons orange juice, 1 teaspoon lime juice, 1/2 teaspoon honey, and a generous 1/4 teaspoon vanilla. Blend until smooth. Serve immediately.

**NUTRITION FACTS:** CALORIES: 129.0 / TOTAL FAT: 1.0 / TRANS FAT: 0.0 / SATURATED FAT: 0.0 / CHOLESTEROL: 21.0 / SODIUM: 39.0 / CARBOHYDRATES: 22.0 / FIBER: 2.0 / SUGAR: 18.0 / PROTEIN: 7.0

# RAINBOW COCONUT SMOOTHIE

| PREP TIME: 10 MINUTES | COOK TIME: NONE | TOTAL TIME: 10 MINUTES | YIELD: 6 (8-OUNCE) SERVINGS |
|---|---|---|---|

### TO PREP

2 tangerines, peeled and segmented

1 cup diced pineapple

1 cup diced mango

1 cup sliced strawberries

1 cup blueberries

1 cup blackberries

1 kiwi, peeled and sliced

2 cups baby spinach

½ cup flaked coconut

### TO SERVE

2 cups coconut water

The more colors we have in our foods, the greater variety of nutrients we're getting. (Although I'm not sure if this applies to rainbow-sprinkled donuts.) And this smoothie has them all!

Let's start with green. Now we all know how amazing spinach is for you: It is the hero of vegetables. But if you don't love spinach, the stunning fruit in this smoothie helps mask the taste.

For the red, blue, and purple, the berries are high in fiber, anti-oxidants, vitamin C, and manganese (a mineral that contributes to healthy bones). Berries are the fruits that keep on giving.

For orange, the clementine packs a punch with its vitamin C content, making this a great smoothie for those winter months. We also have the fun tropical flavors from the mango and the pineapple.

And finally, we have white coconut. Coconut has been on the rise as a must-use food. It's a healthy source of fat that is packed with nutrients that improve lean muscle mass and is also a great source of iron.

1. Combine the tangerines, pineapple, mango, strawberries, blueberries, blackberries, kiwi, spinach, and coconut in a large bowl. Divide among 6 ziplock freezer bags. Freeze for up to a month, until ready to serve.

2. TO MAKE ONE SERVING: Place the contents of one bag in a blender and add ⅓ cup coconut water. Blend until smooth. Serve immediately.

**NUTRITION FACTS:** CALORIES: 184.0 / TOTAL FAT: 0.0 / TRANS FAT: 0.0 / SATURATED FAT: 0.0 / CHOLESTEROL: 0.0 / SODIUM: 114.0 / CARBOHYDRATES: 40.0 / FIBER: 7.0 / SUGAR: 24.0 / PROTEIN: 1.0

# TROPICAL GREEN SMOOTHIE

| PREP TIME: | COOK TIME: | TOTAL TIME: | YIELD: |
|---|---|---|---|
| 5 MINUTES | NONE | 5 MINUTES | 4 (8-OUNCE) SERVINGS |

### TO PREP

4 cups baby spinach

1 cup frozen mango

¾ cup frozen pineapple

1 banana, sliced

2 tangerines, peeled and segmented

4 teaspoons chia seeds

### TO SERVE

3 cups coconut water

Being in LA, there is basically a "healthy" smoothie shop or juice bar on every corner. It's $9.99 for one smoothie, and yes, it's very green and it's very healthy. But it just *tastes* "too healthy"—if you know what I mean.

The hardest part about making a smoothie at home is thinking about what kind of smoothie to make, and then guaranteeing that it's equally healthy and tasty. Because no one wants to drink liquefied spinach at the end of the day.

But don't worry. This tropical green smoothie takes care of both health and taste. The spinach gives you the greens you need, the fruits provide essential vitamins like C and B, and the chia seeds are a superfood rich in fiber and proteins. And it really tastes like a tropical smoothie *without* the liquefied spinach aftertaste.

1. Combine the spinach, mango, pineapple, banana, tangerines, and chia seeds in a large bowl. Divide among 4 ziplock freezer bags. Freeze for up to a month, until ready to serve.

2. TO MAKE ONE SERVING: Place the contents of one bag in a blender and add ¾ cup coconut water. Blend until smooth. Serve immediately.

**NUTRITION FACTS:** CALORIES: 194.0 / TOTAL FAT: 1.0 / TRANS FAT: 0.0 / SATURATED FAT: 0.0 / CHOLESTEROL: 0.0 / SODIUM: 209.0 / CARBOHYDRATES: 42.0 / FIBER: 8.0 / SUGAR: 31.0 / PROTEIN: 3.0

THAI CHICKEN
BUDDHA BOWLS

# 6. Cold Lunch

# CARNITAS MEAL PREP BOWLS

| PREP TIME: | COOK TIME: | TOTAL TIME: | YIELD: |
|---|---|---|---|
| 30 MINUTES | 8 HOURS | 8 ½ HOURS | 8 SERVINGS |

2 ½ teaspoons chili powder

1 ½ teaspoons ground cumin

1 ½ teaspoons dried oregano

1 teaspoon kosher salt, or more to taste

½ teaspoon ground black pepper, or more to taste

1 (3-pound) pork loin, excess fat trimmed

4 cloves garlic, peeled

1 onion, cut into wedges

Juice of 2 oranges

Juice of 2 limes

8 cups shredded kale

4 plum tomatoes, chopped

2 (15-ounce) cans black beans, drained and rinsed

4 cups corn kernels (frozen, canned, or roasted)

2 avocados, halved, pitted, peeled, and diced*

2 limes, cut into wedges

A carnitas meal prep bowl is the fix for your craving for Mexican food, without leaving you with all that heaviness. I mean, when we go out for Mexican food, you can find me in the corner with about ten carnitas tacos. It's not cute.

But don't worry. We're doing this sans tortillas, but with plenty of veggies and only 482 calories per meal prep container.

So how are we doing it? Well, you'll need to dust off that slow cooker to make the most tender carnitas ever. All you need is a simple spice mixture for your pork loin—then, simply set and forget your slow cooker for 8 hours.

Boom. Shred your pork and pack your containers, then serve later with avocado and lime wedges. It is a beautiful rainbow on your plate—and I'm sure your coworker would try to steal a bite, seething in complete jealousy.

1. In a small bowl, combine the chili powder, cumin, oregano, salt, and pepper. Season the pork with the spice mixture, rubbing in thoroughly on all sides.

2. Place the pork, garlic, onion, orange juice, and lime juice in a slow cooker. Cover and cook on low for 8 hours, or on high for 4 to 5 hours.

3. Remove the pork from the cooker and shred the meat. Return it to the pot and toss with the juices; season with salt and pepper, if needed. Cover and keep warm for an additional 30 minutes.

4. Place the pork, kale, tomatoes, black beans, and corn into meal prep containers. Will keep covered in the refrigerator 3 to 4 days. Serve with avocado and lime wedges.

NOTE

* Cut avocado will turn brown when exposed to air, so either prep the avocado just before serving, or brush olive oil or lime or lemon juice over it before placing in the meal prep container.

**NUTRITION FACTS:** CALORIES: 482.0 / TOTAL FAT: 11.0 / TRANS FAT: 0.0 / SATURATED FAT: 3.0 / CHOLESTEROL: 82.0 / SODIUM: 1192.0 / CARBOHYDRATES: 55.0 / FIBER: 13.0 / SUGAR: 7.0 / PROTEIN: 45.0

# CHICAGO HOT DOG SALAD

| PREP TIME: 20 MINUTES | COOK TIME: 5 MINUTES | TOTAL TIME: 25 MINUTES | YIELD: 4 SERVINGS |
|---|---|---|---|

### MUSTARD–POPPY SEED VINAIGRETTE

2 tablespoons extra-virgin olive oil

1½ tablespoons yellow mustard

1 tablespoon red wine vinegar

2 teaspoons poppy seeds

½ teaspoon celery salt

Pinch of sugar

Kosher salt and freshly ground black pepper, to taste

1 cup quinoa

4 reduced-fat turkey hot dogs

3 cups shredded baby kale

1 cup halved cherry tomatoes

⅓ cup diced white onion

¼ cup sport peppers*

8 dill pickle spears (optional)

Every city seems to have a signature food item. And though some cities might have the same favorite food, the way it is eaten often differs.

If you are in Chicago, you have to have a Chicago hot dog. That's just a given. A Chicago dog differs from a New York dog or a Detroit dog in that it is topped with pickles, onions, and mustard. And while, yes, it is okay to indulge when you are in Chicago, it's not so great to eat one on a consistent basis.

So, toss the bun and get ready for a smarter version of the Chicago hot dog. By losing the roll and creating a salad with quinoa, you've already cut your calories in half, with just 334 calories a serving!

1. TO MAKE THE VINAIGRETTE: Whisk together the olive oil, mustard, vinegar, poppy seeds, celery salt, and sugar in a medium bowl. Season with salt and pepper to taste. Cover and refrigerate for 3 to 4 days.

2. Cook the quinoa according to package instructions in a large saucepan with 2 cups water; set aside.

3. Heat a grill to medium-high. Add the hot dogs to the grill and cook until golden brown and lightly charred on all sides, 4 to 5 minutes. Let cool and cut into bite-size pieces.

4. Divide the quinoa, hot dogs, tomatoes, onion, and peppers into meal prep containers. Will keep refrigerated 3 to 4 days.

5. To serve, pour the dressing on top of the salad and gently toss to combine. Serve immediately, garnished with pickle spears, if desired.

**NOTE**
* Sport peppers, typically found on a Chicago-style hot dog, are tangy, medium-heat pickled peppers. Some of you may have never seen or heard of a sport pepper—but others can't have a legit Chicago hot dog without them! They are available in most grocery stores in the pickle aisle.

**NUTRITION FACTS:** CALORIES: 334.0 / TOTAL FAT: 15.0 / TRANS FAT: 0.0 / SATURATED FAT: 3.0 / CHOLESTEROL: 32.0 / SODIUM: 1120.0 / CARBOHYDRATES: 38.0 / FIBER: 6.0 / SUGAR: 5.0 / PROTEIN: 11.0

# FISH TACO BOWLS

| PREP TIME:<br>25 MINUTES | COOK TIME:<br>45 MINUTES | TOTAL TIME:<br>1 HOUR 10 MINUTES | YIELD:<br>4 SERVINGS |
|---|---|---|---|

### CILANTRO LIME DRESSING

1 cup loosely packed cilantro, stems removed

½ cup Greek yogurt

2 cloves garlic,

Juice of 1 lime

Pinch of kosher salt

¼ cup extra-virgin olive oil

2 tablespoons apple cider vinegar

### TILAPIA

3 tablespoons unsalted butter, melted

3 cloves garlic, minced

Grated zest of 1 lime

2 tablespoons freshly squeezed lime juice, or more to taste

4 (4-ounce) tilapia fillets

Kosher salt and freshly ground black pepper, to taste

⅔ cup quinoa

2 cups shredded kale

1 cup shredded red cabbage

1 cup corn kernels (canned or roasted)

2 plum tomatoes, diced

¼ cup crushed tortilla chips*

2 tablespoons chopped fresh cilantro leaves

We all know that here in Southern California, we're famous for our fish tacos. That and traffic congestion, of course. But with this recipe, you don't have to travel farther than your own kitchen for the same SoCal feeling.

Using quinoa instead of rice is a no-brainer. Quinoa is a plant-based source of iron. It's a high-fiber, high-protein grain and super versatile, making it a smart choice with so many meals.

Tilapia is also a great low-calorie source of protein that perfectly complements the garlic, lime, and cilantro. Plus, the addition of vegetables and the cilantro lime dressing will make you feel like you're sitting on a beach in Baja!

1. FOR THE DRESSING: Combine the cilantro, yogurt, garlic, lime juice, and salt in the bowl of a food processor. With the motor running, add the olive oil and vinegar in a slow stream until emulsified. Cover and refrigerate for 3 to 4 days.

2. FOR THE TILAPIA: Preheat the oven to 425 degrees F. Lightly oil a 9x13-inch baking dish or coat with nonstick spray.

3. In a small bowl, whisk together the butter, garlic, lime zest, and lime juice. Season the tilapia with salt and pepper and place in the prepared baking dish. Drizzle with the butter mixture.

4. Bake until the fish flakes easily with a fork, 10 to 12 minutes.

5. Cook the quinoa according to package instructions in a large saucepan with 2 cups water. Let cool.

6. Divide the quinoa into meal prep containers. Top with tilapia, kale, cabbage, corn, tomatoes, and tortilla chips.* Will keep covered in the refrigerator 3 to 4 days. To serve, drizzle with cilantro lime dressing, garnished with cilantro, if desired.

NOTE
* Tortilla chips should be stored in ziplock bags to avoid sogginess of any kind.

NUTRITION FACTS:  CALORIES: 476.0 / TOTAL FAT: 29.0 / TRANS FAT: 0.0 / SATURATED FAT: 11.0 / CHOLESTEROL: 138.0 / SODIUM: 890.0 / CARBOHYDRATES: 21.0 / FIBER: 3.0 / SUGAR: 4.0 / PROTEIN: 33.0

# HARVEST COBB SALAD

| PREP TIME: | COOK TIME: | TOTAL TIME: | YIELD: |
|---|---|---|---|
| 20 MINUTES | 30 MINUTES | 50 MINUTES | 4 SERVINGS |

## POPPY SEED DRESSING

¼ cup 2% milk

3 tablespoons olive oil mayonnaise

2 tablespoons Greek yogurt

1½ tablespoons sugar, or more to taste

1 tablespoon apple cider vinegar

1 tablespoon poppy seeds

2 tablespoons olive oil

16 ounces butternut squash, cut into 1-inch chunks

16 ounces Brussels sprouts, halved

2 sprigs fresh thyme

5 fresh sage leaves

Kosher salt and freshly ground black pepper, to taste

4 medium eggs

4 slices bacon, diced

8 cups shredded kale

1⅓ cups cooked wild rice

In LA, we don't really get a fall season. We don't get the pretty leaves falling, the cool autumn breeze, or the fun light scarves. We basically have 106-degree weather in the middle of October. And then we have 50-degree weather six days later.

But with this Cobb salad, I get to have all the goodness of fall during most of the year, with my favorite poppy seed dressing and perfectly roasted butternut squash and Brussels sprouts. So, go ahead, bring on the 106-degree weather again! I'll be home with the AC and my fall salad. K, thanks!

1. FOR THE DRESSING: Whisk together the milk, mayonnaise, yogurt, sugar, vinegar, and poppy seeds in a small bowl. Cover and refrigerate for up to 3 days.

2. Preheat the oven to 400 degrees F. Lightly oil a baking sheet or coat with nonstick spray.

3. Place the squash and Brussels sprouts on the prepared baking sheet. Add the olive oil, thyme, and sage and gently toss to combine; season with salt and pepper. Arrange in an even layer and bake, turning once, for 25 to 30 minutes, until tender; set aside.

4. Meanwhile, place the eggs in a large saucepan and cover with cold water by 1 inch. Bring to a boil and cook for 1 minute. Cover the pot with a tight-fitting lid and remove from heat; let sit for 8 to 10 minutes. Drain well and let cool before peeling and slicing.

5. Heat a large skillet over medium-high heat. Add the bacon and cook until brown and crispy, 6 to 8 minutes; drain excess fat. Transfer to a paper towel–lined plate; set aside.

6. To assemble the salads, place the kale into meal prep containers; arrange rows of squash, Brussels sprouts, bacon, egg, and wild rice on top. Will keep covered in the refrigerator 3 to 4 days. Serve with the poppy seed dressing.

**NUTRITION FACTS:** CALORIES: 437.0 / TOTAL FAT: 21.0 / TRANS FAT: 0.0 / SATURATED FAT: 5.0 / CHOLESTEROL: 177.0 / SODIUM: 491.0 / CARBOHYDRATES: 39.0 / FIBER: 7.0 / SUGAR: 5.0 / PROTEIN: 19.0

# BUFFALO CAULIFLOWER COBB SALAD

| PREP TIME:<br>20 MINUTES | COOK TIME:<br>20 MINUTES | TOTAL TIME:<br>40 MINUTES | YIELD:<br>4 SERVINGS |
|---|---|---|---|

**GREEK YOGURT RANCH DRESSING**

¼ cup 2% Greek yogurt

2 tablespoons low-fat buttermilk

1 tablespoon mayonnaise (optional)

1 teaspoon freshly squeezed lemon juice

¼ teaspoon dried parsley

¼ teaspoon dried basil

¼ teaspoon dried dill

⅛ teaspoon garlic powder

⅛ teaspoon onion powder

Kosher salt and freshly ground black pepper, to taste

*(continued)*

I feel like a Cobb salad just screams classic lunch salad. But it also screams a ton of calories and a not-so-healthy dressing. I may not be a lady who lunches but I do want a Cobb that isn't going to land like a ton of bricks in my stomach. So I've decided to take a classic salad and give it a modern meal prep twist.

I kept some of the usual suspects: eggs, tomatoes, cucumbers, and lettuce. But instead of the usual meat choice of ham, I used cauliflower here. It makes for a great meat substitute because it's a vegetable that essentially takes on any flavoring or spices you use—in this case, it's buffalo sauce for that nice little punch of heat. Plus, cauliflower is full of vitamins C and K and folate. It is also a great vegetable to eat after working out due to its anti-inflammatory properties.

Ranch dressing is a must-have on your Cobb salad, but it is probably one of the least healthy salad dressings out there. So I've created a much healthier version using Greek yogurt. Same great taste, yet way fewer calories. If you really feel you must have it, you can add a tablespoon of mayonnaise. However, it is not a necessity.

1. TO MAKE THE RANCH DRESSING: Whisk together the yogurt, buttermilk, mayonnaise if using, lemon juice, parsley, basil, dill, garlic powder, and onion powder in a medium bowl; season with salt and pepper to taste. Cover and refrigerate for up to 3 days.

2. TO ROAST THE CAULIFLOWER: Preheat the oven to 425 degrees F. Lightly oil a baking sheet or coat with nonstick spray.

3. In a small bowl, whisk together the Frank's RedHot and butter; set aside. Place the cauliflower florets on the prepared baking sheet. Add the olive oil and garlic and season with salt and pepper. Gently toss to combine. Arrange in a single layer and roast for 12 to 14 minutes, until the cauliflower is tender and golden brown.

*(continued)*

**NUTRITION FACTS:** CALORIES: 331.0 / TOTAL FAT: 24.0 / TRANS FAT: 0.0 / SATURATED FAT: 9.0 / CHOLESTEROL: 199.0 / SODIUM: 1012.0 / CARBOHYDRATES: 17.0 / FIBER: 6.0 / SUGAR: 8.0 / PROTEIN: 13.0

## BUFFALO CAULIFLOWER

¼ cup Frank's RedHot

¼ cup unsalted butter, melted

1 head cauliflower, cut into bite-size florets

2 teaspoons extra-virgin olive oil

2 cloves garlic, minced

Kosher salt and freshly ground black pepper, to taste

4 medium eggs

8 cups chopped romaine lettuce

2 cups cherry tomatoes, halved

2 English cucumbers, peeled and sliced

2 carrots, peeled and grated

4. Pour the Frank's RedHot mixture over the cauliflower and gently toss to combine. Bake for an additional 5 to 7 minutes, until the sauce is bubbling and browned around the edges.

5. Place the eggs in a large saucepan and cover with cold water by 1 inch. Bring to a boil and cook for 1 minute. Cover the pot with a tight-fitting lid and remove from heat; let sit for 8 to 10 minutes. Drain well and let cool before peeling and slicing.

6. To assemble the salad, place the romaine lettuce into meal prep containers;* top with arranged rows of cauliflower, egg, tomatoes, cucumbers, and carrots. Will keep covered in the refrigerator 3 to 4 days.  Serve with Greek yogurt ranch, or desired dressing.

NOTE
* If you're meal prepping several days ahead, the romaine should be stored in ziplock bags to prevent wilting.

# MASON JAR BEET AND BRUSSELS SPROUT GRAIN BOWLS

| PREP TIME: 45 MINUTES | COOK TIME: 45 MINUTES | TOTAL TIME: 1½ HOURS | YIELD: 4 SERVINGS |
|---|---|---|---|

3 medium beets (about 1 pound)

1 tablespoon olive oil

Kosher salt and freshly ground black pepper, to taste

1 cup farro

4 cups baby spinach or kale

2 cups Brussels sprouts (about 8 ounces), thinly sliced

3 clementines, peeled and segmented

½ cup pecans, toasted

½ cup pomegranate seeds

**HONEY-DIJON RED WINE VINAIGRETTE**

¼ cup extra-virgin olive oil

2 tablespoons red wine vinegar

½ shallot, minced

1 tablespoon honey

2 teaspoons whole grain mustard

Kosher salt and freshly ground black pepper, to taste

When Ben, my husband-to-be (who is also known as Butters' dad in the social media world), goes out of town for work, I take a large bowl and I make a kitchen sink salad bowl of all my favorites. It's different every time, but this concoction—which seemed like a random set of ingredients (at first)—actually turned out to be one of my all-time favorites.

I'm obsessed with it. It's bright, it's colorful, and it just feels super light and healthy.

Other than staining your fingertips red, beets are actually kind of incredible. They are packed with vitamins and minerals, help blood pressure, aid in digestion, and protect your liver.

Farro, an ancient grain that is healthy and easily adapts to a ton of recipes, is high in fiber, protein, and iron.

With the greens, I like to switch it up whether I use spinach or kale. They're both superfoods so you can't go wrong. Sometimes I put kale in some bowls and spinach in the others. I know, living on the edge here.

Pecans do not need to be saved for the holidays. With potassium, manganese, zinc, and magnesium, they make a fantastic addition to any salad. Plus, they have monounsaturated fats, which help in lowering cholesterol. They help dress the salad and make it feel a bit heartier.

Pomegranates take this already nutritious meal to another level. They are packed with vitamins C and A, and they add a nice little zest to the overall flavors. So you've got your protein in the farro, a ton of vegetables, and fruit with the pomegranates, see...a true kitchen sink meal in a jar.

1. Preheat the oven to 400 degrees F. Line a baking sheet with foil.

2. Place the beets on the foil, drizzle with olive oil, and season with salt and pepper. Fold up all 4 sides of the foil to make a

*(continued)*

**NUTRITION FACTS:** CALORIES: 532.0 / TOTAL FAT: 27.0 / TRANS FAT: 0.0 / SATURATED FAT: 3.0 / CHOLESTEROL: 0.0 / SODIUM: 423.0 / CARBOHYDRATES: 72.0 / FIBER: 12.0 / SUGAR: 18.0 / PROTEIN: 12.0

pouch. Bake until fork-tender, 35 to 45 minutes; let cool, about 30 minutes.

3. Using a clean paper towel, rub the beets to remove the skins; dice into bite-size pieces.

4. Cook the farro according to package directions, then let cool.

5. Divide the beets into 4 (32-ounce) widemouth glass jars with lids. Top with spinach or kale, farro, Brussels sprouts, clementines, pecans, and pomegranate seeds. Will keep covered in the refrigerator 3 or 4 days.

6. FOR THE VINAIGRETTE: Whisk together the olive oil, vinegar, shallot, honey, mustard, and 1 tablespoon water; season with salt and pepper to taste. Cover and refrigerate for up to 3 days.

7. To serve, add the vinaigrette to each jar and shake. Serve immediately.

# MASON JAR BROCCOLI SALAD

| PREP TIME:<br>15 MINUTES | COOK TIME:<br>NONE | TOTAL TIME:<br>15 MINUTES | YIELD:<br>4 SERVINGS |
|---|---|---|---|

### DRESSING

3 tablespoons 2% milk

2 tablespoons olive oil mayonnaise

2 tablespoons Greek yogurt

1 tablespoon sugar, or more to taste

2 teaspoons apple cider vinegar

½ cup cashews

¼ cup dried cranberries

½ cup diced red onion

2 ounces cheddar cheese, diced

5 cups coarsely chopped broccoli florets

It's a bird, it's a plane, it's super broccoli!

Was that lame? Probably. But broccoli *is* considered a super veggie. It is high in many nutrients, including fiber, vitamin C, vitamin K, iron, and potassium. Broccoli also contains more protein than most other vegetables and is known for fighting cancer and chronic diseases such as heart disease and diabetes. So it is no wonder that a salad centered around broccoli is a smart choice for meal prep. And cashews, full of copper, calcium, magnesium, iron, and zinc, are considered a healthy fat, which helps our bodies absorb vitamins. Plus, they're good for the brain.

The best part? The salad has just 264 calories per serving! Superhero status with minimal calories. Yes and yes.

1. FOR THE DRESSING: Whisk together the milk, mayonnaise, yogurt, sugar, and vinegar in a small bowl.

2. Divide the dressing into 4 (16-ounce) widemouth glass jars with lids. Top with cashews, cranberries, onion, cheese, and broccoli. Refrigerate for up to 3 days.

3. To serve, shake the contents of a jar and serve immediately.

**NUTRITION FACTS:** CALORIES: 264.0 / TOTAL FAT: 16.0 / TRANS FAT: 0.0 / SATURATED FAT: 3.0 / CHOLESTEROL: 10.0 / SODIUM: 137.0 / CARBOHYDRATES: 22.0 / FIBER: 4.0 / SUGAR: 11.0 / PROTEIN: 8.0

# MASON JAR CHICKEN SALAD

| PREP TIME: 20 MINUTES | COOK TIME: NONE | TOTAL TIME: 20 MINUTES | YIELD: 4 SERVINGS |
|---|---|---|---|

2 ½ cups leftover shredded rotisserie chicken

½ cup Greek yogurt

2 tablespoons olive oil mayonnaise

¼ cup diced red onion

1 stalk celery, diced

1 tablespoon freshly squeezed lemon juice, or more to taste

1 teaspoon chopped fresh tarragon

½ teaspoon Dijon mustard

½ teaspoon garlic powder

Kosher salt and freshly ground black pepper, to taste

4 cups shredded kale

2 Granny Smith apples, cored and chopped

½ cup cashews

½ cup dried cranberries

I love a classic chicken salad. There's something about it that just feels like home and comfort. But I have an issue with chicken salad, and that is the amount of mayo that goes into it. Plus, mayo is very high in fat, and I'd rather reserve all the calories I can for my donut-eating habits.

So to reduce some of that fat, I add Greek yogurt and use only 2 tablespoons of mayonnaise. It's so much healthier, and cuts down the calories tremendously without compromising taste! To give you some perspective, get this: There's 747.5 calories in ½ cup of mayonnaise, yet there's only 100 calories in ½ cup of Greek yogurt!

1. In a large bowl, combine the chicken, yogurt, mayonnaise, red onion, celery, lemon juice, tarragon, mustard, and garlic powder; season with salt and pepper to taste.

2. Divide the chicken mixture into 4 (24-ounce) widemouth glass jars with lids. Top with kale, apples, cashews, and cranberries. Refrigerate for up to 3 days.

3. To serve, shake contents of a jar and serve immediately.

**NUTRITION FACTS:** CALORIES: 380.0 / TOTAL FAT: 13.0 / TRANS FAT: 0.0 / SATURATED FAT: 3.0 / CHOLESTEROL: 102.0 / SODIUM: 625.0 / CARBOHYDRATES: 36.0 / FIBER: 5.0 / SUGAR: 18.0 / PROTEIN: 34.0

# MASON JAR CHINESE CHICKEN SALAD

| PREP TIME: | COOK TIME: | TOTAL TIME: | YIELD: |
|---|---|---|---|
| 15 MINUTES | NONE | 15 MINUTES | 4 SERVINGS |

## VINAIGRETTE

½ cup rice wine vinegar

2 cloves garlic, pressed

1 tablespoon sesame oil

1 tablespoon freshly grated ginger

2 teaspoons sugar, or more to taste

½ teaspoon reduced-sodium soy sauce

2 green onions, thinly sliced

1 teaspoon sesame seeds

2 carrots, peeled and grated

2 cups diced English cucumber

2 cups shredded purple cabbage

12 cups chopped kale

1½ cups leftover diced rotisserie chicken

1 cup wonton strips

One of the best salads ever is the Chinese chicken salad. It's so basic, and nothing too crazy or out of the ordinary, but it really is the best. Plus, we have so many goodies here.

First and foremost, we have the superfood kale. A typical Chinese chicken salad uses Napa cabbage, but kale holds up much better and is stronger for our meal prep needs. And you guys know how good kale is for you.

I prefer using English cucumbers over regular cucumbers. They don't have as many seeds and taste a bit sweeter.

Purple cabbage is best in its raw form for retaining vitamins and minerals, making it a great addition to any salad. It contains fiber, as well as potassium and vitamins A and C.

But the true best part about this salad is the crunchy wonton strips. This is what makes the salad really shine. I mean, there is just something so satisfying about having a little extra crunch in your food.

So here's one of my personal favorites in mason jar form for all your lunch needs. Simply shake and serve.

1. FOR THE VINAIGRETTE: Whisk together the vinegar, garlic, sesame oil, ginger, sugar, and soy sauce in a small bowl. Divide the dressing into 4 (32-ounce) widemouth glass jars with lids.

2. Top with green onions, sesame seeds, carrots, cucumber, cabbage, kale, and chicken. Refrigerate for up to 3 days. Store the wonton strips separately.

3. To serve, shake contents of a jar and add the wonton strips. Serve immediately.

**NUTRITION FACTS:** CALORIES: 375.0 / TOTAL FAT: 11.0 / TRANS FAT: 0.0 / SATURATED FAT: 1.0 / CHOLESTEROL: 98.0 / SODIUM: 691.0 / CARBOHYDRATES: 35.0 / FIBER: 5.0 / SUGAR: 4.0 / PROTEIN: 40.0

# MASON JAR NIÇOISE SALAD

| PREP TIME:<br>20 MINUTES | COOK TIME:<br>10 MINUTES | TOTAL TIME:<br>30 MINUTES | YIELD:<br>4 SERVINGS |
| --- | --- | --- | --- |

2 medium eggs

2½ cups halved green beans

3 (7-ounce) cans albacore tuna packed in water, drained and rinsed

¼ cup extra-virgin olive oil

2 tablespoons red wine vinegar

2 tablespoons diced red onion

2 tablespoons chopped fresh parsley leaves

1 tablespoon chopped fresh tarragon leaves

1½ teaspoons Dijon mustard

Kosher salt and freshly ground black pepper, to taste

1 cup halved cherry tomatoes

4 cups torn butter lettuce

3 cups arugula leaves

12 kalamata olives

1 lemon, cut into wedges (optional)

Okay, true story: I didn't know anything about Niçoise salads until I watched *White Chicks,* which is kind of like the funniest movie ever. One of the girls was trying to tell a joke about how your mother is so stupid that she mispronounced Niçoise salad. Except nobody laughed in the movie.

I didn't laugh either. I thought, *Wait, what is that?*

When I did finally learn about the salad, I only found it at bourgeois, fancy-schmancy hotel restaurants where you pay $25 for a half plate of salad with a little bit of tuna.

But here is my budget-friendly mason jar spin on it instead. First off, we have so many fun features here, like green beans, eggs, cherry tomatoes, butter lettuce, arugula, olives, and albacore tuna. But don't let the myths of canned tuna deceive you. Albacore tuna is actually a rich source of protein. It is also a very economical protein option when you stock up on those cans during sale time! There's no need to pay $25 for this at a stuffy restaurant!

1. Place the eggs in a large saucepan and cover with cold water by 1 inch. Bring to a boil and cook for 1 minute. Cover the pot with a tight-fitting lid and remove from the heat; let sit for 8 to 10 minutes.

2. Meanwhile, in a large pot of boiling salted water, blanch the green beans until bright green in color, about 2 minutes. Drain and cool in a bowl of ice water. Drain well. Drain the eggs and let cool before peeling and cutting the eggs in half lengthwise.

3. In a large bowl, combine the tuna, olive oil, vinegar, onion, parsley, tarragon, and Dijon until just combined; season with salt and pepper to taste.

4. Divide the tuna mixture into 4 (32-ounce) widemouth glass jars with lids. Top with green beans, eggs, tomatoes, butter lettuce, arugula, and olives. Refrigerate for up to 3 days.

5. To serve, shake contents of a jar. Serve immediately, with lemon wedges if desired.

**NUTRITION FACTS:** CALORIES: 310.0 / TOTAL FAT: 17.0 / TRANS FAT: 0.0 / SATURATED FAT: 3.0 / CHOLESTEROL: 126.0 / SODIUM: 536.0 / CARBOHYDRATES: 12.0 / FIBER: 4.0 / SUGAR: 3.0 / PROTEIN: 25.0

# SPICY TUNA BOWLS

| PREP TIME: 20 MINUTES | COOK TIME: 45 MINUTES | TOTAL TIME: 1 HOUR 5 MINUTES | YIELD: 4 SERVINGS |
|---|---|---|---|

1 cup long-grain brown rice

3 tablespoons olive oil mayonnaise

3 tablespoons Greek yogurt

1 tablespoon sriracha sauce, or more to taste

1 tablespoon lime juice

2 teaspoons reduced-sodium soy sauce

2 (5-ounce) cans albacore tuna, drained and rinsed

Kosher salt and freshly ground black pepper, to taste

2 cups shredded kale

1 tablespoon toasted sesame seeds

2 teaspoons toasted sesame oil

1½ cups diced English cucumber

½ cup pickled ginger

3 green onions, thinly sliced

½ cup shredded roasted nori

So I kind of love a spicy tuna roll. I know; it's so basic. But I can't help it. I love it so much, I used to have gas station spicy tuna rolls back in the day. I was on a college budget, so gas station food had to work for me at the time. Except, once I did get a round of food poisoning from a tuna roll, so I think I learned my lesson.

But don't worry. I found a budget-friendly *and* stomach-friendly alternative.

It's spicy tuna bowls using canned albacore tuna! Believe it or not, albacore tuna has many nutritional advantages: It's a rich source of complete protein and vitamin $B_{12}$, plus, it's a far better source of heart-healthy omega-3 fatty acids than other tuna species.

As for rice, when choosing between brown and white, I prefer brown rice as it is a whole grain that is high in fiber and low in calories.

Then we have the kale, which we know is an amazing superfood that hasn't wavered in popularity. It is great for digestion, high in vitamins B and C, and promotes iron absorption, which is essential for the on-the-go lifestyles that we all have.

1. Cook the rice according to package instructions in 2 cups water in a medium saucepan; set aside.

2. In a small bowl, whisk together the mayonnaise, yogurt, sriracha, lime juice, and soy sauce. Spoon 2 tablespoons of the mayonnaise mixture into a second bowl, cover, and refrigerate. Stir the tuna into the remaining mayo mixture and gently toss to combine; season with salt and pepper to taste.

3. In a medium bowl, combine the kale, sesame seeds, and sesame oil; season with salt and pepper to taste.

4. Divide the rice into meal prep containers. Top with tuna mixture, kale mixture, cucumber, ginger, green onions, and nori. Refrigerate for up to 3 days.

5. To serve, drizzle with the mayonnaise mixture.

**NUTRITION FACTS:** CALORIES: 392.0 / TOTAL FAT: 14.0 / TRANS FAT: 0.0 / SATURATED FAT: 2.0 / CHOLESTEROL: 23.0 / SODIUM: 688.0 / CARBOHYDRATES: 47.0 / FIBER: 4.0 / SUGAR: 7.0 / PROTEIN: 13.0

# STEAK COBB SALAD

| PREP TIME: | COOK TIME: | TOTAL TIME: | YIELD: |
| --- | --- | --- | --- |
| 30 MINUTES | 15 MINUTES | 45 MINUTES | 4 SERVINGS |

## BALSAMIC VINAIGRETTE

3 tablespoons extra-virgin olive oil

4 1/2 teaspoons balsamic vinegar

1/4 teaspoon sugar, or more to taste

1 clove garlic, pressed

1 1/2 teaspoons dried parsley flakes

1/4 teaspoon dried basil

1/4 teaspoon dried oregano

1/4 teaspoon Dijon mustard (optional)

4 medium eggs

1 tablespoon unsalted butter

12 ounces steak

2 teaspoons olive oil

Kosher salt and freshly ground black pepper, to taste

8 cups baby spinach

2 cups cherry tomatoes, halved

1/2 cup pecan halves

1/2 cup crumbled reduced-fat feta cheese

This is one of my favorite winter meals for when the weather gets a little colder, the air a bit crisper, and sweaters a bit chunkier. And I just want to state for the record, when I say chunky sweaters, I mean Butters' sweaters. Not mine.

No, but really, can we talk about this salad though? This salad is complete comfort food without any of the comfort food calories. And it's also one of those $18 restaurant salads without actually costing $18!

You can use your choice of New York strip, rib-eye, or filet mignon, or a more cost-effective cut, if you like. Any should work just fine.

An added bonus is the pecans. They are high in healthy unsaturated fat, and just a handful a day can lower bad cholesterol.

So grab your cable knit dog sweaters (yeah, it's a thing!), your steak, and your pecans and enjoy the cool weather!

1. FOR THE BALSAMIC VINAIGRETTE: Whisk together the olive oil, balsamic vinegar, sugar, garlic, parsley, basil, oregano, and mustard (if using) in a medium bowl. Cover and refrigerate for up to 3 days.

2. Place the eggs in a large saucepan and cover with cold water by 1 inch. Bring to a boil and cook for 1 minute. Cover the pot with a tight-fitting lid and remove from heat; let sit for 8 to 10 minutes. Drain well and let cool before peeling and slicing.

3. Melt the butter in a large skillet over medium-high heat. Using paper towels, pat both sides of the steak dry. Drizzle with the olive oil and season with salt and pepper. Add the steak to the skillet and cook, flipping once, until cooked through to desired doneness, 3 to 4 minutes per side for medium-rare. Let rest 10 minutes before cutting into bite-size pieces.

4. To assemble the salads, place spinach into meal prep containers; top with arranged rows of steak, eggs, tomatoes, pecans, and feta. Cover and refrigerate for up to 3 days. Serve with the balsamic vinaigrette or desired dressing.

**NUTRITION FACTS:** CALORIES: 490.0 / TOTAL FAT: 35.0 / TRANS FAT: 0.0 / SATURATED FAT: 9.0 / CHOLESTEROL: 242.0 / SODIUM: 736.0 / CARBOHYDRATES: 9.0 / FIBER: 3.0 / SUGAR: 3.0 / PROTEIN: 34.0

# SWEET POTATO NOURISH BOWLS

| PREP TIME: | COOK TIME: | TOTAL TIME: | YIELD: |
|:---:|:---:|:---:|:---:|
| 20 MINUTES | 30 MINUTES | 50 MINUTES | 4 SERVINGS |

2 medium sweet potatoes, peeled and cut into 1-inch chunks

3 tablespoons extra-virgin olive oil, divided

½ teaspoon smoked paprika

Kosher salt and freshly ground black pepper, to taste

1 cup farro

1 bunch lacinato kale, shredded

1 tablespoon freshly squeezed lemon juice

1 cup shredded red cabbage

1 cup halved cherry tomatoes

¾ cup Crispy Garbanzo Beans (from Kale Chips Snack Box, page 175)

2 avocados, halved, pitted, and peeled*

So, what I really love about this bowl is that it repurposes so many ingredients from the other recipes in this book. You should have leftover farro, kale, and cabbage from the Thai Chicken Buddha Bowls (page 113), and you can use the crispy garbanzo beans from the Kale Chips Snack Box (page 175). And if you've made the Stuffed Sweet Potatoes—4 Ways (page 150), you should have an abundance of sweet potatoes around.

So, there you go. I just took care of 87 percent of the ingredient list right there. Now, we have a glowing nourish bowl with basically only two or three ingredients you may actually need. So there's no excuses not to make this, right?

1. Preheat the oven to 400 degrees F. Line a baking sheet with parchment paper.

2. Place the sweet potatoes on the prepared baking sheet. Add 1½ tablespoons of the olive oil and the paprika, season with salt and pepper, and gently toss to combine. Arrange in a single layer and bake for 20 to 25 minutes, turning once, until easily pierced with a fork.

3. Cook the farro according to package instructions; set aside.

4. Combine the kale, lemon juice, and the remaining 1½ tablespoons olive oil in a medium bowl. Massage the kale until well combined and season with salt and pepper to taste.

5. Divide farro into meal prep containers. Top with sweet potatoes, cabbage, tomatoes, and crispy garbanzos. Refrigerate for up to 3 days. Serve with the avocado.

**NOTE**
* Cut avocado will turn brown when exposed to air, so either prep the avocado just before serving, or brush olive oil or lime or lemon juice over it before placing in the meal prep container.

**NUTRITION FACTS:** CALORIES: 479.0 / TOTAL FAT: 21.0 / TRANS FAT: 0.0 / SATURATED FAT: 3.0 / CHOLESTEROL: 0.0 / SODIUM: 241.0 / CARBOHYDRATES: 72.0 / FIBER: 17.0 / SUGAR: 9.0 / PROTEIN: 13.0

# THAI CHICKEN BUDDHA BOWLS

| PREP TIME:<br>20 MINUTES | COOK TIME:<br>30 MINUTES | TOTAL TIME:<br>50 MINUTES | YIELD:<br>4 SERVINGS |
|---|---|---|---|

**SPICY PEANUT SAUCE**

3 tablespoons creamy peanut butter

2 tablespoons freshly squeezed lime juice

1 tablespoon reduced-sodium soy sauce

2 teaspoons dark brown sugar

2 teaspoons sambal oelek (ground fresh chile paste)

1 cup farro

¼ cup chicken stock

1½ tablespoons sambal oelek (ground fresh chile paste)

1 tablespoon light brown sugar

1 tablespoon freshly squeezed lime juice

1 pound boneless, skinless chicken breasts, cut into 1-inch chunks

1 tablespoon cornstarch

1 tablespoon fish sauce

1 tablespoon olive oil

2 cloves garlic, minced

1 shallot, minced

1 tablespoon freshly grated ginger

Kosher salt and freshly ground black pepper, to taste

*(continued)*

Now you might ask, what exactly is a Buddha bowl? There seems to be a million definitions but this is what I came across: Also called "glory bowl" or "hippie bowl," a Buddha bowl is a colorful bowl filled with tons of greens, veggies, beans, and a healthy grain—all in all, loaded with tons of nutrients and vitamins.

So that's basically what we have here, guys (well, at least my version):

- **Whole grain—farro.** Farro is a far superior whole grain with more protein and fiber than, say, brown rice.
- **Protein—chicken.** Boneless, skinless chicken breast is low in fat and calories and high in protein, which makes it ideal for weight maintenance. It is also jam-packed with essential nutrients and vitamins.
- **Vegetables—kale, cabbage, bean sprouts, carrots.** We have a rainbow of veggies here, which basically means: The more colors you have, the more nutrients you're getting.
- **Bonus—best peanut sauce ever.**

Traditional Buddha bowls are made sans meat, but they have since evolved into a broader definition. You can certainly sub in a plant-based protein for the chicken, if that's what you prefer.

But really, the most important point to remember is this: The peanut sauce is absolute LIFE. That is all.

1. FOR THE PEANUT SAUCE: Whisk together the peanut butter, lime juice, soy sauce, brown sugar, sambal oelek, and 2 to 3 tablespoons water in a small bowl. Cover and refrigerate for up to 3 days.

2. Cook the farro according to package instructions; set aside.

3. While the farro cooks, in a small bowl, whisk together the stock, sambal oelek, brown sugar, and lime juice; set aside.

*(continued)*

NUTRITION FACTS: CALORIES: 503.0 / TOTAL FAT: 18.0 / TRANS FAT: 0.0 / SATURATED FAT: 3.0 / CHOLESTEROL: 68.0 / SODIUM: 1103.0 / CARBOHYDRATES: 61.0 / FIBER: 4.0 / SUGAR: 6.0 / PROTEIN: 28.0

**2 cups shredded kale**

**1½ cups shredded purple cabbage**

**1 cup bean sprouts**

**2 carrots, peeled and grated**

**½ cup fresh cilantro leaves**

**¼ cup roasted peanuts**

4. In a large bowl, combine the chicken, cornstarch, and fish sauce, toss to coat, and let the chicken absorb the cornstarch for a few minutes.

5. Heat the olive oil in a large skillet over medium heat. Add the chicken and cook until golden, 3 to 5 minutes. Add the garlic, shallot, and ginger and continue to cook, stirring frequently, until fragrant, about 2 minutes. Stir in the stock mixture and cook until slightly thickened, about 1 minute. Season with salt and pepper to taste.

6. Divide the farro into meal prep containers. Top with chicken, kale, cabbage, bean sprouts, carrots, cilantro, and peanuts. Will keep covered in the refrigerator 3 to 4 days. Serve with the spicy peanut sauce.

# THAI PEANUT CHICKEN WRAPS

| PREP TIME:<br>20 MINUTES | COOK TIME:<br>NONE | TOTAL TIME:<br>20 MINUTES | YIELD:<br>4 SERVINGS |
|---|---|---|---|

## COCONUT CURRY PEANUT SAUCE

¼ cup light coconut milk

3 tablespoons creamy peanut butter

1½ tablespoons seasoned rice wine vinegar

1 tablespoon reduced-sodium soy sauce

2 teaspoons dark brown sugar

1 teaspoon chili garlic sauce

¼ teaspoon yellow curry powder

2½ cups leftover diced rotisserie chicken

2 cups shredded Napa cabbage

1 cup thinly sliced red bell pepper

2 carrots, peeled and cut into matchsticks

1½ tablespoons freshly squeezed lime juice

1 tablespoon olive oil mayonnaise

Kosher salt and freshly ground black pepper, to taste

3 ounces reduced-fat cream cheese, at room temperature

1 teaspoon freshly grated ginger

4 (8-inch) sun-dried tomato tortilla wraps

Let's just say it. Starbucks has kind of mastered lunch-on-the-go. But who can afford to buy one every single day of the week? This is a cheaper, budget-friendly, copycat version of their super popular Thai peanut chicken wrap.

Each ingredient of the wrap has its own flavoring, making it a delectable combination. And be sure to make the coconut peanut sauce beforehand so you can put it in the fridge to chill. But before you do, reserve about 3 tablespoons of the sauce to marinate the chicken.

Once you have made your wraps, put them in the meal prep containers along with your coconut peanut sauce. When I know I am going to use this as a meal prep for a few days or if I am taking it on the go, I like to put my sauce in a small plastic container as well. Compartmentalizing is everything.

Now you can enjoy your coffee shop favorites every day with this light but filling meal, full of healthy ingredients like carrots, bell peppers, and ginger.

1. FOR THE COCONUT CURRY PEANUT SAUCE: Whisk together the coconut milk, peanut butter, rice wine vinegar, soy sauce, brown sugar, chili garlic sauce, and curry powder in a small bowl. Set aside 3 tablespoons for the chicken; refrigerate the remainder until ready to serve.

2. In a large bowl, combine the chicken and the 3 tablespoons peanut sauce and toss until coated.

3. In a medium bowl, combine the cabbage, bell pepper, carrots, lime juice, and mayonnaise; season with salt and pepper to taste.

*(continued)*

**NUTRITION FACTS:** CALORIES: 491.0 / TOTAL FAT: 22.0 / TRANS FAT: 0.0 / SATURATED FAT: 6.0 / CHOLESTEROL: 91.0 / SODIUM: 1250.0 / CARBOHYDRATES: 37.0 / FIBER: 5.0 / SUGAR: 7.0 / PROTEIN: 37.0

4. In a small bowl, combine the cream cheese and ginger; season with salt and pepper to taste.

5. Spread the cream cheese mixture evenly on the tortillas, leaving a 1-inch border. Top with the chicken and the cabbage mixture. Fold in sides by about 1 inch, then roll up tightly from the bottom. Will keep covered in the refrigerator 3 to 4 days. Serve each wrap with coconut curry peanut sauce.

# TURKEY SPINACH PINWHEELS

| PREP TIME: | COOK TIME: | TOTAL TIME: | YIELD: |
| --- | --- | --- | --- |
| 15 MINUTES | NONE | 15 MINUTES | 1 SERVING |

1 slice cheddar cheese

2 ounces thinly sliced turkey breast

½ cup baby spinach

1 (8-inch) spinach tortilla

6 baby carrots

¼ cup grapes

5 cucumber slices

I love a good pinwheel. They remind me of my weekend trips to Price Club, aka Costco. Is there anyone else who still says Price Club—or is it just me? Anyway, the Costco pinwheels. They come in one of those giant plastic party platters and cost like $1.99 or something insane. It gave me life. And I probably ate 20 or so pinwheels at a time.

The point of this story was to tell you that this is not your typical Costco pinwheel. We get a bit fancier here using a spinach tortilla, turkey, and cheese. Although I wouldn't mind a schmear of hummus . . . or ranch.

But hey, at 400 calories per box, I can't complain.

1. Place the cheese, turkey, and spinach in the center of the tortilla. Bring the bottom edge of the tortilla tightly over the spinach and fold in the sides. Roll up until the top of the tortilla is reached. Cut into 6 pinwheels.

2. Place pinwheels, carrots, grapes, and cucumber slices into a meal prep container. Keeps covered in the refrigerator for 2 to 3 days.

NUTRITION FACTS: CALORIES: 400.0 / TOTAL FAT: 13.0 / TRANS FAT: 0.0 / SATURATED FAT: 7.0 / CHOLESTEROL: 73.0 / SODIUM: 842.0 / CARBOHYDRATES: 40.0 / FIBER: 3.0 / SUGAR: 11.0 / PROTEIN: 28.0

# TURKEY TACO SALAD

| PREP TIME: | COOK TIME: | TOTAL TIME: | YIELD: |
|:---:|:---:|:---:|:---:|
| 20 MINUTES | 10 MINUTES | 30 MINUTES | 4 SERVINGS |

1 tablespoon olive oil

1½ pounds ground turkey*

1 (1.25-ounce) package taco seasoning

8 cups shredded romaine lettuce

½ cup pico de gallo (homemade or store-bought)

½ cup Greek yogurt

½ cup shredded Mexican cheese blend

1 lime, cut into wedges

Low-Carb Taco Tuesdays!!! Okay, it's not really a mainstream thing, but it's catching on. I promise. Plus, this salad is so perfect and hearty, you won't miss the taco shells. I mean, you will, but you won't miss them *that* much.

With the crumbled ground turkey, pico de gallo, Greek yogurt (instead of sour cream—you're welcome, guys), cheese, and a lime wedge, we have plenty going on here!

1. Heat the olive oil in a large skillet over medium-high heat. Add the ground turkey and cook until browned, 3 to 5 minutes, making sure to crumble the meat as it cooks; stir in the taco seasoning. Drain excess fat.

2. Place the romaine lettuce in sandwich bags. Place the pico de gallo, yogurt, and cheese into separate 2-ounce Jell-O-shot cups with lids. Put it all—the turkey, romaine, pico de gallo, yogurt, cheese, and lime wedges—into meal prep containers.** Will keep covered in the refrigerator 3 to 4 days.

**NOTES**
\* Ground chicken, pork, or beef can be substituted for the turkey.
\*\*There is nothing worse than a soggy taco. By individually packing each ingredient in its own airtight container, you ensure a super fresh meal prep!

**NUTRITION FACTS:** CALORIES: 349.0 / TOTAL FAT: 21.0 / TRANS FAT: 0.0 / SATURATED FAT: 8.0 / CHOLESTEROL: 105.0 / SODIUM: 807.0 / CARBOHYDRATES: 410.0 / FIBER: 6.0 / SUGAR: 3.0 / PROTEIN: 30.0

# VERY GREEN MASON JAR SALAD

| PREP TIME: | COOK TIME: | TOTAL TIME: | YIELD: |
|---|---|---|---|
| 20 MINUTES | 45 MINUTES | 1 HOUR 5 MINUTES | 4 SERVINGS |

¾ cup pearled barley

1 cup fresh basil leaves

¾ cup 2% Greek yogurt

2 green onions, chopped

1½ tablespoons freshly squeezed lime juice

1 clove garlic, peeled

Kosher salt and freshly ground black pepper, to taste

½ English cucumber, coarsely chopped

1 pound (4 small) zucchini, spiralized

4 cups shredded kale

1 cup frozen green peas, thawed

½ cup crumbled reduced-fat feta cheese

½ cup pea shoots

1 lime, cut into wedges (optional)

This is my "New Year, New You" January salad. That is, after I've consumed all the ham, scalloped potatoes, and pancetta cornbread stuffing I could possible fit into my 5-foot 0-inch body during the winter holidays.

So I try my best to eat all that is green. I mean, between the kale, peas, and zucchini, you've got vitamins A, C, K, and B all covered. You've also got your minerals like calcium, magnesium, potassium, zinc, and iron—and even protein.

Plus, you can't feel bad about eating this at all. It's 250 calories and you still get to have cheese. It's a win-win detox situation here.

1. Cook the barley according to package instructions; let cool completely and set aside.

2. To make the dressing, combine the basil, yogurt, green onions, lime juice, and garlic in the bowl of a food processor and season with salt and pepper. Pulse until smooth, about 30 seconds to 1 minute.

3. Divide the dressing into 4 (32-ounce) widemouth glass jars with lids. Top with cucumber, zucchini noodles, barley, kale, peas, feta, and pea shoots. Refrigerate for up to 3 days.

4. To serve, shake the contents in a jar. Serve immediately, with lime wedges, if desired.

**NUTRITION FACTS:** CALORIES: 250.0 / TOTAL FAT: 3.0 / TRANS FAT: 0.0 / SATURATED FAT: 2.0 / CHOLESTEROL: 22.0 / SODIUM: 384.0 / CARBOHYDRATES: 38.0 / FIBER: 6.0 / SUGAR: 8.0 / PROTEIN: 13.0

# ZUCCHINI SPRING ROLL BOWLS WITH SPICY PEANUT SAUCE

| PREP TIME: 30 MINUTES | COOK TIME: 5 MINUTES | TOTAL TIME: 35 MINUTES | YIELD: 4 SERVINGS |
| --- | --- | --- | --- |

## SPICY PEANUT SAUCE

- 3 tablespoons creamy peanut butter
- 2 tablespoons freshly squeezed lime juice
- 1 tablespoon reduced-sodium soy sauce
- 2 teaspoons dark brown sugar
- 2 teaspoons sambal oelek (ground fresh chile paste)

- 1 pound medium shrimp, peeled and deveined
- 4 medium zucchini, spiralized
- 2 large carrots, peeled and grated
- 2 cups shredded purple cabbage
- ⅓ cup fresh cilantro leaves
- ⅓ cup basil leaves
- ¼ cup mint leaves
- ¼ cup chopped roasted peanuts

If I had to pick one appetizer for the rest of my life, it would be the spring roll. Maybe just because they always come with the best peanut dressing. But the trickiest part to making them at home is conquering the rice paper. So instead of trying to skillfully wrap all those vegetables in fragile rice paper, I just threw everything into one convenient bowl.

I also swapped out the typical noodles for zucchini spirals. Zucchini has fewer carbs and less sugar, with more nutrients. Win, win, and win. And between the mint, basil, and cilantro, your lunch will be bursting with so many flavors.

You can swap out the shrimp for chicken—or even tofu if you want a meatless meal. This is honestly one of the best meal preps during those hot summer months when you don't want a heavy meal weighing you down. You want something light and refreshing but still enough to fill you up—with just 266 calories per serving!

1. FOR THE PEANUT SAUCE: Whisk together the peanut butter, lime juice, soy sauce, brown sugar, sambal oelek, and 2 to 3 tablespoons water in a small bowl. Refrigerate for up to 3 days, until ready to serve.

2. In a large pot of boiling salted water, cook the shrimp until pink, about 3 minutes. Drain and cool in a bowl of ice water. Drain well.

3. Divide zucchini into meal prep containers. Top with shrimp, carrots, cabbage, cilantro, basil, mint, and peanuts. Will keep covered in the refrigerator 3 to 4 days. Serve with the spicy peanut sauce.

**NUTRITION FACTS:** CALORIES: 266.0 / TOTAL FAT: 14.0 / TRANS FAT: 0.0 / SATURATED FAT: 2.0 / CHOLESTEROL: 177.0 / SODIUM: 912.0 / CARBOHYDRATES: 20.0 / FIBER: 6.0 / SUGAR: 12.0 / PROTEIN: 21.0

MASON JAR BOLOGNES

# 7. Warm Lunch

# CHICKEN BURRITO BOWLS

| PREP TIME: | COOK TIME: | TOTAL TIME: | YIELD: |
|------------|------------|-------------|--------|
| 20 MINUTES | 40 MINUTES | 1 HOUR | 4 SERVINGS |

## CHIPOTLE CREAM SAUCE

½ cup nonfat Greek yogurt

1 chipotle pepper in adobo sauce, minced, or more to taste

1 clove garlic, minced

1 tablespoon freshly squeezed lime juice

⅔ cup brown rice

1 tablespoon olive oil

1 pound ground chicken

½ teaspoon chili powder

½ teaspoon garlic powder

½ teaspoon ground cumin

½ teaspoon dried oregano

¼ teaspoon onion powder

¼ teaspoon paprika

Kosher salt and freshly ground black pepper, to taste

1 (15-ounce) can black beans, drained and rinsed

1¾ cups corn kernels (frozen, canned, or roasted)

½ cup pico de gallo (homemade or store-bought)

¼ cup fresh cilantro leaves (optional)

1 lime, cut into wedges (optional)

Let's be honest, burritos are legit bomb.com. But if I ate a burrito every time I wanted one, you would have to roll me around to go anywhere. Thankfully, there is a perfect solution to this burrito crisis: Enter the 488-calorie chicken burrito bowl: all the burrito goodness without any of the guilt.

But guys, it's the chipotle sauce that will really send you over the edge here. I use Greek yogurt for this because it's just that much healthier and I can always use an extra probiotic or two. The chipotle pepper in adobo sauce contributes smoky flavor, and you can add as much or as little as you like.

I am telling you, this healthier version of a burrito makes it an easy choice to add to your meal prep rotation!

1. FOR THE CHIPOTLE CREAM SAUCE: Whisk together the yogurt, chipotle pepper, garlic, and lime juice. Cover and refrigerate for up to 3 days.

2. Cook the rice according to package instructions in a large saucepan with 2 cups water; set aside.

3. Heat the olive oil in a large stockpot or Dutch oven over medium-high heat. Add the ground chicken, chili powder, garlic powder, cumin, oregano, onion powder, and paprika; season with salt and pepper. Cook until the chicken has browned, 3 to 5 minutes, making sure to crumble the chicken as it cooks; drain excess fat.

4. Divide rice into meal prep containers. Top with ground chicken mixture, black beans, corn, and pico de gallo. Will keep covered in the refrigerator for 3 to 4 days. Drizzle with chipotle cream sauce. Garnish with cilantro and lime wedge, if desired, and serve. Reheat in the microwave in 30-second intervals until heated through.

**NUTRITION FACTS:** CALORIES: 488.0 / TOTAL FAT: 9.0 / TRANS FAT: 0.0 / SATURATED FAT: 2.0 / CHOLESTEROL: 100.0 / SODIUM: 1163.0 / CARBOHYDRATES: 55.0 / FIBER: 11.0 / SUGAR: 6.0 / PROTEIN: 43.0

# CHICKEN TIKKA MASALA

| PREP TIME: 20 MINUTES | COOK TIME: 25 MINUTES | TOTAL TIME: 45 MINUTES | YIELD: 4 SERVINGS |
| --- | --- | --- | --- |

1 cup basmati rice

2 tablespoons unsalted butter

1½ pounds boneless, skinless chicken breasts, cut into 1-inch chunks

Kosher salt and freshly ground black pepper, to taste

1 onion, diced

2 tablespoons tomato paste

1 tablespoon freshly grated ginger

3 cloves garlic, minced

2 teaspoons garam masala*

2 teaspoons chili powder

2 teaspoons ground turmeric

1 (28-ounce) can diced tomatoes

1 cup chicken stock

⅓ cup heavy cream

1 tablespoon fresh lemon juice

¼ cup chopped fresh cilantro leaves (optional)

1 lemon, cut into wedges (optional)

When I was in college, I worked part-time as a receptionist in an optometry office in Beverly Hills. I made close to minimum wage and had a lot of student loans, which meant I was basically eating PB&J for lunch every single day.

Once a month, I would allow myself to indulge in my favorite chicken tikka masala at an Indian restaurant on our street, S. Beverly Drive.

Fast-forward eight years, and this place closed down! I was devastated. I still am. To cope, I've been drowning my sorrows in these homemade tikka bowls. And you know? I think they might taste better than what I remember from all those years ago.

1. Cook the rice according to package instructions in a large saucepan with 2 cups water; set aside.

2. Melt the butter in a large skillet over medium heat. Season the chicken with salt and pepper. Add the chicken and onion to the skillet and cook, stirring occasionally, until golden, 4 to 5 minutes. Stir in the tomato paste, ginger, garlic, garam masala, chili powder, and turmeric and cook until well combined, 1 to 2 minutes. Stir in the diced tomatoes and chicken stock. Bring to a boil; reduce the heat and simmer, stirring occasionally, until slightly thickened, about 10 minutes.

3. Stir in the cream, lemon juice, and chicken and cook until heated through, about 1 minute.

4. Place the rice and chicken mixture into meal prep containers. Garnish with cilantro and lemon wedge, if desired, and serve. Will keep covered in the refrigerator 3 to 4 days. Reheat in the microwave in 30-second intervals until heated through.

NOTE
* Garam masala, an Indian spice mix, is available in most grocery stores.

NUTRITION FACTS: CALORIES: 479.0 / TOTAL FAT: 16.0 / TRANS FAT: 0.0 / SATURATED FAT: 9.0 / CHOLESTEROL: 134.0 / SODIUM: 1001.0 / CARBOHYDRATES: 43.0 / FIBER: 3.0 / SUGAR: 7.0 / PROTEIN: 34.0

# GREEK CHICKEN BOWLS

| PREP TIME: | COOK TIME: | TOTAL TIME: | YIELD: |
|---|---|---|---|
| 1 HOUR | 30 MINUTES | 1½ HOURS | 4 SERVINGS |

### CHICKEN AND RICE

1 pound boneless, skinless chicken breasts

¼ cup plus 2 tablespoons olive oil, divided

3 cloves garlic, minced

Juice of 1 lemon

1 tablespoon red wine vinegar

1 tablespoon dried oregano

Kosher salt and freshly ground black pepper, to taste

¾ cup brown rice

### CUCUMBER SALAD

2 English cucumbers, peeled and sliced

½ cup thinly sliced red onion

Juice of 1 lemon

2 tablespoons extra-virgin olive oil

1 tablespoon red wine vinegar

2 cloves garlic, pressed

½ teaspoon dried oregano

*(continued)*

One of my favorite restaurants in all of LA is this little Greek restaurant at the Grove. We go there for birthdays, for other celebrations, or just when we really need to eat our body weight in hummus.

In fact, my friends took me there the day my first cookbook was released. After we ate all the hummus we could, we ordered these to-die-for Greek chicken salad bowls. They're light, they're fresh, and they're simply perfect.

So, after *plenty* of research and development at this restaurant (the things I do for you guys), I re-created a favorite. Except I made it a little lighter and a little bit heartier. Plus, you know I couldn't let this go without my favorite tzatziki sauce.

1. FOR THE CHICKEN: In a gallon-size ziplock bag, combine the chicken, ¼ cup of the olive oil, the garlic, lemon juice, vinegar, and oregano; season with salt and pepper. Marinate the chicken in the refrigerator for at least 20 minutes or up to 1 hour, turning the bag occasionally. Drain the chicken and discard the marinade.

2. Heat the remaining 2 tablespoons olive oil in a large skillet over medium-high heat. Add the chicken and cook, flipping once, until cooked through, 3 to 4 minutes per side. Let cool before dicing into bite-size pieces.

3. Cook the rice in a large saucepan with 2 cups water according to package instructions.

4. Divide the rice and chicken into meal prep containers. Will keep covered in the refrigerator up to 3 days.

5. FOR THE CUCUMBER SALAD: Combine the cucumbers, onion, lemon juice, olive oil, vinegar, garlic, and oregano in a small bowl. Cover and refrigerate for up to 3 days.

*(continued)*

NUTRITION FACTS: CALORIES: 502.0 / TOTAL FAT: 27.0 / TRANS FAT: 0.0 / SATURATED FAT: 6.0 / CHOLESTEROL: 73.0 / SODIUM: 526.0 / CARBOHYDRATES: 35.0 / FIBER: 3.0 / SUGAR: 9.0 / PROTEIN: 30.0

**TZATZIKI SAUCE**

1 cup Greek yogurt

1 English cucumber, finely diced

2 cloves garlic, pressed

1 tablespoon chopped fresh dill

1 teaspoon grated lemon zest

1 tablespoon freshly squeezed lemon juice

1 teaspoon chopped fresh mint (optional)

Kosher salt and freshly ground black pepper, to taste

2 tablespoons extra-virgin olive oil

$1\frac{1}{2}$ pounds cherry tomatoes, halved

6. *FOR THE TZATZIKI SAUCE:* Combine the yogurt, cucumber, garlic, dill, lemon zest and juice, and mint (if using) in a small bowl. Season with salt and pepper to taste and drizzle with the olive oil. Cover and refrigerate for at least 10 minutes, allowing the flavors to meld. Can be refrigerated 3 to 4 days.

7. To serve, reheat rice and chicken in the microwave in 30-second intervals, until heated through. Top with cucumber salad, tomatoes, and tzatziki sauce and serve.

# KOREAN MEAL PREP BEEF BOWLS

| PREP TIME:<br>20 MINUTES | COOK TIME:<br>20 MINUTES FOR WHITE RICE,<br>40 MINUTES FOR BROWN RICE | TOTAL TIME:<br>40 MINUTES TO 1 HOUR | YIELD:<br>4 SERVINGS |
|---|---|---|---|

2/3 cup white or brown rice

4 medium eggs

1 tablespoon olive oil

2 cloves garlic, minced

4 cups chopped spinach

**KOREAN BEEF**

3 tablespoons packed brown sugar

3 tablespoons reduced-sodium soy sauce

1 tablespoon freshly grated ginger

1½ teaspoons sesame oil

½ teaspoon sriracha (optional)

2 teaspoons olive oil

2 cloves garlic, minced

1 pound ground beef

2 green onions, thinly sliced (optional)

¼ teaspoon sesame seeds (optional)

I traveled to Korea this past year doing my personal version of *Eat, Pray, Love,* a journey from a movie that I actually have never seen. BUT. That's not the point. I made it to Korea and I completely fell in love with the cuisine all over again. It's no wonder that Korean BBQ restaurants are popping up all over the place in the U.S.—the food is pretty darn good. And no, I'm not biased because I'm a Korean-American. Well, maybe a little!

A Korean staple is their Korean beef. The classic consists of a bowl of rice, beef, and side dishes to accompany it. This meal prep is just that, with a few tweaks to make it easier and quicker to prepare. The rice is what takes the longest to cook, so you can imagine just how easy this dish really is.

With traditional Korean BBQ, the meat that is used is called *bulgogi,* which is usually thinly sliced sirloin. I used ground beef instead because it's easier to prepare and easier on your wallet, too.

This has the same classic Korean spices in a typical bulgogi dish, like soy sauce, garlic, brown sugar, and ginger. I also like adding a little sriracha for a bit of heat, but you can pass on that if you prefer.

1. Cook the rice according to package instructions; set aside.

2. Place the eggs in a large saucepan and cover with cold water by 1 inch. Bring to a boil and cook for 1 minute. Cover the pot with a tight-fitting lid and remove from the heat; let sit for 8 to 10 minutes. Drain well and let cool before peeling and slicing in half.

3. Heat the olive oil in a large skillet over medium-high heat. Add the garlic and cook, stirring frequently, until fragrant, 1 to 2 minutes. Stir in the spinach and cook until wilted, 2 to 3 minutes; set aside.

4. For the beef: In a small bowl, whisk together the brown sugar, soy sauce, ginger, sesame oil, and sriracha, if using.

*(continued)*

**NUTRITION FACTS:** CALORIES: 516.0 / TOTAL FAT: 25.0 / TRANS FAT: 0.0 / SATURATED FAT: 6.0 / CHOLESTEROL: 236.0 / SODIUM: 1030.0 / CARBOHYDRATES: 41.0 / FIBER: 4.0 / SUGAR: 12.0 / PROTEIN: 32.0

5. Heat the olive oil in a large skillet over medium-high heat. Add the garlic and cook, stirring constantly, until fragrant, about 1 minute. Add the ground beef and cook until browned, 3 to 5 minutes, making sure to crumble the beef as it cooks; drain excess fat. Stir in the soy sauce mixture and the green onions until well combined, then simmer until heated through, about 2 minutes.

6. Place rice, eggs, spinach, and ground beef mixture into meal prep containers and garnish with green onion and sesame seeds, if desired. Will keep covered in the refrigerator 3 to 4 days. Reheat in the microwave in 30-second intervals until heated through.

# MASON JAR CHICKEN AND RAMEN SOUP

| PREP TIME:<br>30 MINUTES | COOK TIME:<br>5 MINUTES | TOTAL TIME:<br>35 MINUTES | YIELD:<br>4 SERVINGS |
| --- | --- | --- | --- |

2 (5.6-ounce) packages refrigerated yakisoba noodles,* seasoning sauce packets discarded

2½ tablespoons reduced-sodium vegetable broth base concentrate (we like Better Than Bouillon)

1½ tablespoons reduced-sodium soy sauce

1 tablespoon rice wine vinegar

1 tablespoon freshly grated ginger

2 teaspoons sambal oelek (ground fresh chile paste), or more to taste

2 teaspoons sesame oil

2 cups leftover shredded rotisserie chicken

3 cups baby spinach

2 carrots, peeled and grated

1 cup sliced shiitake mushrooms

½ cup fresh cilantro leaves

2 green onions, thinly sliced

1 teaspoon sesame seeds

Cup Noodles was a staple in our home. I think it's a staple in most Korean households. There are just so many varieties and tastes to choose from, and all you do is add boiling water. They are also a staple for many college students, myself included. Unfortunately, they are also laden with sodium and are high in calories. But don't worry, guys. I found a DIY instant version with fewer calories, less preservatives, and less "instant" ingredients—if you know what I mean.

Instead of all those dehydrated vegetables typically found in the seasoning packets, we're using real chicken, fresh spinach, carrots, mushrooms, cilantro, green onions, and sesame seeds!

Yet we're not sacrificing the convenience of Cup Noodles. To serve, simply add hot water and microwave for 2 to 3 minutes. That's it!

1. In a large pot of boiling water, cook the yakisoba until loosened, 1 to 2 minutes; drain well.

2. In a small bowl, combine the broth base, soy sauce, vinegar, ginger, sambal oelek, and sesame oil.

3. Divide the broth mixture into 4 (24-ounce) widemouth glass jars with lids, or other heatproof containers. Top with yakisoba, chicken, spinach, carrots, mushrooms, cilantro, green onions, and sesame seeds. Cover and refrigerate for up to 4 days.

4. To serve, uncover a jar and add enough hot water to cover the contents, about 1¼ cups. Microwave, uncovered, until heated through, 2 to 3 minutes. Let stand 5 minutes, stir to combine, and serve immediately.

NOTE
* Yakisoba are ramen-style noodles that can be found in the refrigerated section of your local grocery store, such as Maruchan Yaki-Soba.

NUTRITION FACTS: CALORIES: 324.0 / TOTAL FAT: 12.0 / TRANS FAT: 0.0 / SATURATED FAT: 3.0 / CHOLESTEROL: 86.0 / SODIUM: 867.0 / CARBOHYDRATES: 31.0 / FIBER: 2.0 / SUGAR: 1.0 / PROTEIN: 23.0

# MASON JAR BOLOGNESE

| PREP TIME: | COOK TIME: | TOTAL TIME: | YIELD: |
|---|---|---|---|
| 30 MINUTES | 8 HOURS 10 MINUTES | 8 HOURS 40 MINUTES | 16 SERVINGS |

2 tablespoons olive oil

1 pound ground beef

1 pound Italian sausage, casings removed

1 onion, minced

4 cloves garlic, minced

3 (14.5-ounce) cans diced tomatoes, drained

2 (15-ounce) cans tomato sauce

3 bay leaves

1 teaspoon dried oregano

1 teaspoon dried basil

½ teaspoon dried thyme

1 teaspoon kosher salt

½ teaspoon freshly ground black pepper

2 (16-ounce) packages reduced-fat mozzarella cheese, cubed

32 ounces uncooked whole wheat fusilli, cooked according to package instructions; about 16 cups cooked

This is batch cooking in all of its glory. With this, you can actually make 16 mason jar meals! Or you can freeze half of the sauce and use 8 portions right away. The sauce will actually keep in the freezer for 3 to 6 months!

Once your sauce is made, go ahead and assemble your jars with your desired pasta (although I highly recommend the whole wheat fusilli) and mozzarella cheese.

Simply microwave and serve. It's basically a little jar of Italy right here. Well, almost.

1. Heat the olive oil in a large skillet over medium-high heat. Add the ground beef, sausage, onion, and garlic. Cook until browned, 5 to 7 minutes, making sure to crumble the beef and sausage as it cooks; drain excess fat.

2. Transfer the ground beef mixture to a 6-quart slow cooker. Stir in the tomatoes, tomato sauce, bay leaves, oregano, basil, thyme, salt, and pepper. Cover and cook on low heat for 7 hours and 45 minutes. Remove the lid and turn the slow cooker to high. Continue to cook for 15 minutes, until the sauce has thickened. Discard the bay leaves and let the sauce cool completely.

3. Divide sauce into 16 (24-ounce) widemouth glass jars with lids, or other heatproof containers. Top with mozzarella and fusilli. Refrigerate for up to 4 days.

4. To serve, microwave, uncovered, until heated through, about 2 minutes. Stir to combine.

**NUTRITION FACTS:** CALORIES: 499.0 / TOTAL FAT: 23.0 / TRANS FAT: 0.0 / SATURATED FAT: 10.0 / CHOLESTEROL: 63.0 / SODIUM: 1078.0 / CARBOHYDRATES: 46.0 / FIBER: 5.0 / SUGAR: 6.0 / PROTEIN: 25.0

# MASON JAR LASAGNA

| PREP TIME:<br>20 MINUTES | COOK TIME:<br>50 MINUTES | TOTAL TIME:<br>1 HOUR 10 MINUTES | YIELD:<br>4 SERVINGS |
|---|---|---|---|

3 lasagna noodles

1 tablespoon olive oil

½ pound ground sirloin

1 onion, diced

2 cloves garlic, minced

3 tablespoons tomato paste

1 teaspoon Italian seasoning

2 (14.5-ounce) cans diced tomatoes

1 medium zucchini, grated

1 large carrot, grated

2 cups shredded baby spinach

Kosher salt and freshly ground black pepper, to taste

1 cup part-skim ricotta cheese

1 cup shredded mozzarella cheese, divided

2 tablespoons chopped fresh basil leaves

Okay, I'm sorry—but who doesn't love a classic lasagna? It's pasta, it's cheese, it's tomato sauce. There's nothing to *not* like here. But my issue is that a large casserole is simply too much for two people. I mean, don't get me wrong; we inhale the leftovers. But portion control just goes out the window in this scenario.

Hence, we have the solution to all of our problems: individual lasagna servings. They're great for portion control, for serving, and for lunchtime because they reheat in just 2 to 3 minutes. Plus, these bad boys are packed with ground sirloin, zucchini, carrots, spinach, and part-skim ricotta. But don't worry. Between all the protein and veggies, you won't notice a difference eating this perfectly portioned 464 calories of homemade comfort food.

1.  In a large pot of boiling salted water, cook the pasta according to package instructions; drain well. Cut each noodle into 4 pieces; set aside.

2.  Heat the olive oil in a large skillet or Dutch oven over medium-high heat. Add the ground sirloin and onion and cook until browned, 3 to 5 minutes, making sure to crumble the beef as it cooks; drain excess fat.

3.  Stir in the garlic, tomato paste, and Italian seasoning and cook until fragrant, 1 to 2 minutes. Stir in the tomatoes, reduce the heat, and simmer until slightly thickened, 5 to 6 minutes. Stir in the zucchini, carrot, and spinach and cook, stirring frequently, until tender, 2 to 3 minutes. Season with salt and pepper to taste. Set sauce aside.

4.  In a small bowl, combine the ricotta, ½ cup of the mozzarella, and the basil; season with salt and pepper to taste.

*(continued)*

**NUTRITION FACTS:** CALORIES: 464.0 / TOTAL FAT: 23.0 / TRANS FAT: 0.0 / SATURATED FAT: 11.0 / CHOLESTEROL: 77.0 / SODIUM: 899.0 / CARBOHYDRATES: 40.0 / FIBER: 8.0 / SUGAR: 11.0 / PROTEIN: 31.0

5. Preheat the oven to 375 degrees F. Lightly oil 4 (16-ounce) widemouth glass jars with lids, or other oven-safe containers, or coat with nonstick spray.

6. Place 1 pasta piece into each jar. Divide one-third of the sauce into the jars. Repeat with a second layer of pasta and sauce. Top with ricotta mixture, remaining pasta, and remaining sauce. Sprinkle with remaining $1/2$ cup mozzarella cheese.

7. Set the jars on a baking sheet. Place in the oven and bake until bubbling, 25 to 30 minutes; cool completely. Refrigerate for up to 4 days.

8. To serve, microwave, uncovered, until heated through, 2 to 3 minutes.

# MASON JAR SHEPHERD'S PIE

| PREP TIME:<br>20 MINUTES | COOK TIME:<br>1 HOUR | TOTAL TIME:<br>1 HOUR 20 MINUTES | YIELD:<br>4 SERVINGS |
| --- | --- | --- | --- |

1½ pounds russet potatoes, peeled and cut into 2-inch chunks

¾ cup 2% milk, plus more if needed

¼ cup light sour cream

Kosher salt and freshly ground black pepper, to taste

1 tablespoon olive oil

12 ounces ground sirloin

8 ounces cremini mushrooms, quartered

1 onion, diced

1 carrot, diced

1 stalk celery, diced

2 tablespoons tomato paste

3 cloves garlic, minced

3 tablespoons all-purpose flour

2 cups beef broth

2 teaspoons Worcestershire sauce

1 teaspoon dried thyme

2 cups chopped kale

¾ cup frozen peas

To me, shepherd's pie screams a comfort food classic. You know, the day you wear that chunky sweater with the giant sweatpants while stuffing your face with all that is good in life.

I know, it sounds too good to be part of the meal prep train.

But don't worry. This shepherd's pie can really make for a great meal prep with only 362 calories per serving.

See, potatoes have a bad rap for being a starchy filler food, but they are actually not so bad. They are a great source of vitamins $B_6$ and C, and magnesium. They also have twice as much potassium as a banana. Plus, given that we are using them as a meal prep, the portion size is actually kind of perfect!

Not to mention, these bad boys are also loaded with tons of veggies, like mushrooms, onion, carrot, celery, kale, and peas!

1. Place the potatoes in a large stockpot or Dutch oven, cover with cold water, and bring to a boil. Reduce the heat, cover, and simmer until the potatoes are tender, 10 to 12 minutes. Drain well and return to the pot.

2. Off heat, add the milk and sour cream and season with salt and pepper. Using an electric mixer fitted with the paddle attachment, blend the potatoes until light and fluffy, 2 to 3 minutes. If the mixture is too thick, add more milk as needed until desired consistency is reached.

3. Heat the olive oil in a large skillet over medium-high heat. Add the ground sirloin and cook until browned, 3 to 5 minutes, making sure to crumble the beef as it cooks; drain excess fat. Stir in the mushrooms, onion, carrot, and celery. Cook, stirring frequently, until tender, 4 to 5 minutes. Stir in the tomato paste and garlic and cook until fragrant, about 1 minute.

*(continued)*

NUTRITION FACTS: CALORIES: 362.0 / TOTAL FAT: 10.0 / TRANS FAT: 0.0 / SATURATED FAT: 4.0 / CHOLESTEROL: 53.0 / SODIUM: 969.0 / CARBOHYDRATES: 45.0 / FIBER: 3.0 / SUGAR: 7.0 / PROTEIN: 23.0

4.  Whisk in the flour until lightly browned, 1 to 2 minutes. Stir in the broth, Worcestershire, and thyme and bring to a boil. Reduce the heat and simmer, stirring occasionally, until thickened and reduced, about 15 minutes.

5.  Add the kale and peas and cook until the kale has wilted, about 2 minutes; season with salt and pepper to taste.

6.  Preheat the oven to 375 degrees F.

7.  Divide the beef mixture into 4 (16-ounce) widemouth glass jars with lids, or other oven-safe containers. Top with potatoes.

8.  Set the jars on a baking sheet. Place in the oven and bake until bubbling, 20 to 25 minutes; cool completely. Refrigerate for up to 4 days.

9.  To serve, microwave, uncovered, until heated through, 2 to 3 minutes.

# MISO GINGER DETOX SOUP

| PREP TIME:<br>15 MINUTES | COOK TIME:<br>20 MINUTES | TOTAL TIME:<br>35 MINUTES | YIELD:<br>6 SERVINGS (10 CUPS) |
|---|---|---|---|

2 teaspoons toasted sesame oil

2 teaspoons canola oil

3 cloves garlic, minced

1 tablespoon freshly grated ginger

6 cups vegetable stock

1 sheet kombu,* cut into small pieces

4 teaspoons white miso paste

1 (3.5-ounce) package shiitake mushrooms, sliced (about 2 cups)

8 ounces firm tofu, cubed

5 baby bok choy, chopped

¼ cup sliced green onions

Miso soup is always a must during a sushi run. Its aroma, warmth, and flavor make it the perfect start to any meal. So, I decided to bring it home, but I wanted more than your average miso soup.

This detox soup keeps the simplicity of a traditional miso soup, but it adds a ton more flavor and health benefits. What a lot of people don't realize is that miso aids in digestion and provides protein and vitamins $B_{12}$, K, and E.

Kombu, otherwise known as seaweed, can be found in most grocery stores. It is an edible kelp that is full of minerals and nutrients. It is also high in iron, which is crucial to healthy body function and preventing anemia. Bok choy is a Chinese cabbage that is really flavorful and abundant in nutrients. It is high in vitamin A, which is crucial for maintaining a healthy immune system.

So whether it is a cold winter day, or you are trying to recover from an illness, or you just want a healthy meal, this soup fulfills all those needs at 97 calories per bowl.

1. Heat the sesame oil and canola oil in a large stockpot or Dutch oven over medium heat. Add the garlic and ginger and cook, stirring frequently, until fragrant, 1 to 2 minutes. Stir in the stock, kombu, and miso paste and bring to a boil. Cover, reduce the heat, and simmer for 10 minutes. Stir in the mushrooms and cook until tender, about 5 minutes.

2. Stir in the tofu and bok choy and cook until the tofu is heated through and the bok choy is just tender, about 2 minutes. Stir in the green onions. Serve immediately.

3. Or, to prep ahead of time, let the stock cool completely at the end of step 1. Then stir in the tofu, bok choy, and green onions. Divide into airtight containers, cover, and refrigerate for up to 3 days. To reheat, place in the microwave in 30-second intervals until heated through.

**NOTE**
*Kombu can be found at Whole Foods.

**NUTRITION FACTS:** CALORIES: 97.0 / TOTAL FAT: 6.0 / TRANS FAT: 0.0 / SATURATED FAT: 0.0 / CHOLESTEROL: 0.0 / SODIUM: 945.0 / CARBOHYDRATES: 5.0 / FIBER: 1.0 / SUGAR: 3.0 / PROTEIN: 5.0

# STUFFED SWEET POTATOES— 4 WAYS

For the longest time, I thought the only way to eat sweet potatoes was in the form of fries. My favorite burger joint, Father's Office, makes the best basket of sweet potato fries and serves them with a heavenly garlic aioli. That's basically how I consumed sweet potatoes for about seven years of my adult life.

But little did I know, sweet potatoes are incredibly versatile, packed with disease-preventing, cancer-fighting, and immune-boosting benefits. Loaded with fiber as well as vitamins A and C, one cooked medium sweet potato has only 103 calories and 2.3 grams of protein!

Here are four of my favorite ways to enjoy this superfood.

## ROASTED SWEET POTATOES

| PREP TIME: 5 MINUTES | COOK TIME: 1 HOUR 10 MINUTES | TOTAL TIME: 1¼ HOURS | YIELD: 4 SERVINGS |
|---|---|---|---|

**4 medium sweet potatoes**

1. Preheat the oven to 400 degrees F. Line a baking sheet with parchment paper or aluminum foil.
2. Place the sweet potatoes in a single layer on the prepared baking sheet. Bake until fork-tender, about 1 hour and 10 minutes.
3. Let rest until cool enough to handle.

# Korean Chicken Stuffed Potatoes

| PREP TIME:<br>45 MINUTES | COOK TIME:<br>10 MINUTES | TOTAL TIME:<br>55 MINUTES | YIELD:<br>4 SERVINGS |
|---|---|---|---|

½ cup seasoned rice wine vinegar

1 tablespoon sugar

Kosher salt and freshly ground black pepper, to taste

1 cup matchstick carrots

1 large shallot, sliced

¼ teaspoon crushed red pepper flakes

2 teaspoons sesame oil

1 (10-ounce) package fresh spinach

2 cloves garlic, minced

4 roasted sweet potatoes (page 150)

2 cups Spicy Korean Sesame Chicken (page 247)

This is a great way to repurpose leftovers from the Meal Prep Chicken—3 Ways (page 247). Hello, extra protein!

1. In a small saucepan, combine the vinegar, sugar, 1 teaspoon salt, and ¼ cup water. Bring to a boil over medium heat. Stir in the carrots, shallot, and red pepper flakes. Remove from the heat and let stand 30 minutes.

2. Heat the sesame oil in a large skillet over medium heat. Stir in the spinach and garlic and cook until the spinach has wilted, 2 to 4 minutes. Season with salt and pepper to taste.

3. Halve the potatoes lengthwise and season with salt and pepper. Top with the chicken, carrot mixture, and spinach.

4. Divide the sweet potatoes into meal prep containers. Refrigerate for up to 3 days. Reheat in the microwave in 30-second intervals until heated through.

**NUTRITION FACTS:** CALORIES: 378.0 / TOTAL FAT: 14.0 / TRANS FAT: 0.0 / SATURATED FAT: 2.0 / CHOLESTEROL: 65.0 / SODIUM: 1068.0 / CARBOHYDRATES: 42.0 / FIBER: 5.0 / SUGAR: 17.0 / PROTEIN: 22.0

# Kale and Red Pepper Stuffed Potatoes

| PREP TIME: | COOK TIME: | TOTAL TIME: | YIELD: |
|---|---|---|---|
| **15 MINUTES** | **10 MINUTES** | **25 MINUTES** | **4 SERVINGS** |

1 tablespoon olive oil

2 cloves garlic, minced

1 sweet onion, diced

1 teaspoon smoked paprika

1 red bell pepper, thinly sliced

1 bunch curly kale, stems removed and leaves chopped

Kosher salt and freshly ground black pepper, to taste

4 roasted sweet potatoes (page 150)

½ cup crumbled reduced-fat feta cheese

With only 198 calories per loaded sweet potato, sometimes I have two potatoes for dinner—because I'm pretty sure I saw a tank top in the gym that said *Kale is the new carbs.*

1. Heat the olive oil in a large skillet over medium heat. Add the garlic and onion and cook, stirring frequently, until the onion is translucent, 2 to 3 minutes. Stir in the paprika and cook until fragrant, about 30 seconds.

2. Stir in the bell pepper and cook until crisp-tender, about 2 minutes. Stir in the kale, a handful at a time, and cook until bright green and just wilted, 3 to 4 minutes. Season with salt and pepper to taste.

3. Halve the potatoes lengthwise and season with salt and pepper. Top with the kale mixture and feta.

4. Divide the sweet potatoes into meal prep containers. Refrigerate for up to 3 days. Reheat in the microwave in 30-second intervals until heated through.

**NUTRITION FACTS:** CALORIES: 198.0 / TOTAL FAT: 6.0 / TRANS FAT: 0.0 / SATURATED FAT: 2.0 / CHOLESTEROL: 7.0 / SODIUM: 420.0 / CARBOHY-DRATES: 30.0 / FIBER: 6.0 / SUGAR: 8.0 / PROTEIN: 7.0

# Honey-Mustard Chicken Stuffed Potatoes

| PREP TIME: 15 MINUTES | COOK TIME: 10 MINUTES | TOTAL TIME: 25 MINUTES | YIELD: 4 SERVINGS |
|---|---|---|---|

1 tablespoon olive oil

2 cups cut fresh green beans

1½ cups quartered cremini mushrooms

1 shallot, minced

1 clove garlic, minced

2 tablespoons chopped fresh parsley leaves

Kosher salt and freshly ground black pepper, to taste

4 roasted sweet potatoes (page 150)

2 cups Honey Mustard Chicken (page 250)

Just like the Korean chicken potatoes, you can use up leftover Meal Prep Chicken here. You also get an extra dose of veggies with the green beans and mushrooms.

1. Heat the olive oil in a large skillet over medium heat. Add the green beans, mushrooms, and shallot and cook, stirring frequently, until the green beans are crisp-tender, 5 to 6 minutes. Stir in the garlic and parsley and cook until fragrant, about 1 minute. Season with salt and pepper to taste.

2. Halve the potatoes lengthwise and season with salt and pepper. Top with the green bean mixture and chicken.

3. Divide the sweet potatoes into meal prep containers. Refrigerate for up to 3 days. Reheat in the microwave in 30-second intervals until heated through.

**NUTRITION FACTS:** CALORIES: 379.0 / TOTAL FAT: 14.0 / TRANS FAT: 0.0 / SATURATED FAT: 3.0 / CHOLESTEROL: 65.0 / SODIUM: 822.0 / CARBOHY-DRATES: 41.0 / FIBER: 6.0 / SUGAR: 18.0 / PROTEIN: 24.0

# Black Bean and Pico de Gallo Stuffed Potatoes

| PREP TIME: 20 MINUTES | COOK TIME: 20 MINUTES | TOTAL TIME: 40 MINUTES | YIELD: 4 SERVINGS |
|---|---|---|---|

## BLACK BEANS

1 tablespoon olive oil

½ sweet onion, diced

1 clove garlic, minced

1 teaspoon chili powder

½ teaspoon ground cumin

1 (15.5-ounce) can black beans, rinsed and drained

1 teaspoon apple cider vinegar

Kosher salt and freshly ground black pepper, to taste

## PICO DE GALLO

2 plum tomatoes, diced

½ sweet onion, diced

1 jalapeño, seeded and minced

3 tablespoons chopped fresh cilantro leaves

1 tablespoon freshly squeezed lime juice

Kosher salt and freshly ground black pepper, to taste

4 roasted sweet potatoes (page 150)

1 avocado, halved, pitted, peeled, and diced*

¼ cup light sour cream

I reserve these potatoes for my Taco Tuesdays! Sometimes I even crush a few tortilla chips on top. Ben, on the other hand, tops his off with the entire bag of tortilla chips!

1. FOR THE BEANS: Heat the olive oil in a medium saucepan over medium heat. Add the onion and cook, stirring frequently, until translucent, 2 to 3 minutes. Stir in the garlic, chili powder, and cumin and cook until fragrant, about 1 minute.

2. Stir in the beans and ⅔ cup water. Bring to a simmer, reduce the heat, and cook until reduced, 10 to 15 minutes. Using a potato masher, mash the beans until smooth and desired consistency is reached. Stir in the vinegar and season with salt and pepper to taste.

3. FOR THE PICO DE GALLO: Combine the tomatoes, onion, jalapeño, cilantro, and lime juice in a medium bowl. Season with salt and pepper to taste.

4. Halve the potatoes lengthwise and season with salt and pepper. Top with the black bean mixture and pico de gallo.

5. Divide the sweet potatoes into meal prep containers. Refrigerate for up to 3 days. Reheat in the microwave in 30-second intervals until heated through.

6. Serve with avocado and sour cream.

### NOTE
*Cut avocado will turn brown when exposed to air, so either prep the avocado just before serving, or brush olive oil or lime or lemon juice over it before placing in the meal prep container.

**NUTRITION FACTS:** CALORIES: 312.0 / TOTAL FAT: 11.0 / TRANS FAT: 0.0 / SATURATED FAT: 3.0 / CHOLESTEROL: 6.0 / SODIUM: 360.0 / CARBOHYDRATES: 46.0 / FIBER: 12.0 / SUGAR: 10.0 / PROTEIN: 9.0

# ZUCCHINI NOODLES WITH TURKEY MEATBALLS

| PREP TIME: | COOK TIME: | TOTAL TIME: | YIELD: |
|---|---|---|---|
| 1 HOUR | 20 MINUTES | 1 HOUR 20 MINUTES | 4 SERVINGS |

## MEATBALLS

1 pound ground turkey

1/3 cup panko*

3 tablespoons freshly grated Parmesan

2 large egg yolks

3/4 teaspoon dried oregano

3/4 teaspoon dried basil

1/2 teaspoon dried parsley

1/4 teaspoon garlic powder

1/4 teaspoon crushed red pepper flakes

Kosher salt and freshly ground black pepper, to taste

2 pounds (3 medium) zucchini, spiralized

2 teaspoons kosher salt

2 cups marinara sauce (homemade or store-bought)

1/4 cup freshly grated Parmesan cheese

How about we trade in our carb-loaded pasta for something that's low-carb, low-calorie, and full of veggies. That's right! We're trading it in for zucchini noodles!

Using zucchini means instead of all the sugar and carbs, you will be loading up on vitamins A and C. It is also a great source of fiber and potassium, and has been known to improve heart health.

And when you compare 2 cups of pasta with 2 cups of zucchini noodles, pasta has 480 calories, 90 grams of carbs, and 2 grams of fiber, while the latter has 66 calories, 12 grams of carbs, and 4 grams of fiber. So we have 13 percent of the calories and twice the fiber? Um, yes, please!

1. Preheat the oven to 400 degrees F. Lightly oil a 9x13-inch baking dish or coat with nonstick spray.

2. In a large bowl, combine the ground turkey, panko, Parmesan, egg yolks, oregano, basil, parsley, garlic powder, and red pepper flakes; season with salt and pepper. Using a wooden spoon or clean hands, mix until well combined. Roll the mixture into 16 to 20 meatballs, each 1 to 1 1/2 inches in diameter.

3. Place the meatballs in the prepared baking dish and bake for 15 to 18 minutes, until browned all over and cooked through; set aside.

4. Place the zucchini in a colander over the sink. Add the salt and gently toss to combine; let sit for 10 minutes. In a large pot of boiling water, cook the zucchini for 30 seconds to 1 minute; drain well.

5. Divide the zucchini into meal prep containers. Top with meatballs, marinara sauce, and Parmesan. Will keep covered in the refrigerator 3 to 4 days. Reheat in the microwave, uncovered, in 30-second intervals until heated through.

### NOTE
* Panko is Japanese-style breadcrumbs that can be found in the Asian section of your local grocery store.

**NUTRITION FACTS:** CALORIES: 221.0 / TOTAL FAT: 9.0 / TRANS FAT: 0.0 / SATURATED FAT: 3.0 / CHOLESTEROL: 230.0 / SODIUM: 2111.0 / CARBOHYDRATES: 19.0 / FIBER: 3.0 / SUGAR: 10.0 / PROTEIN: 17.0

# 8. Snacks

# ANTIPASTO SNACK BOX FOR TWO

| PREP TIME:<br>10 MINUTES | COOK TIME:<br>NONE | TOTAL TIME:<br>10 MINUTES | YIELD:<br>2 SERVINGS |
| --- | --- | --- | --- |

2 ounces thinly sliced prosciutto

2 ounces salami, cubed

1 ounce gouda cheese, thinly sliced

1 ounce Parmesan cheese, thinly sliced

¼ cup Marcona almonds

2 tablespoons green olives

2 tablespoons black olives

Before my company Damn Delicious really took off, it was just a hobby. I had a nine-to-five job, working at a variety of different doctor's offices—dermatology, optometry, and orthodontia.

The days would feel really long, and lunch breaks were tough. I would try to save as much money as I possibly could and would often resort to that $5 footlong at Subway.

But on the days I could splurge, I would make a mini "cheese board" for me and my coworker, Kristie. We'd rush to the break room, as we only had 30 minutes to inhale all the salami and cheese we possibly could. Anything we didn't finish, we'd have at the end of the workday with a bottle of red wine. Those were truly the best workdays.

So if you have a favorite coworker whom you share a cubicle with, go ahead and bring in this snack box. She'll love you forever and ever.

1. Place prosciutto, salami, cheeses, almonds, and olives in a meal prep container. Cover and refrigerate for up to 4 days.

**NUTRITION FACTS:** CALORIES: 310.0 / TOTAL FAT: 24.0 / TRANS FAT: 0.0 / SATURATED FAT: 9.0 / CHOLESTEROL: 56.0 / SODIUM: 1641.0 / CARBOHYDRATES: 3.0 / FIBER: 0.0 / SUGAR: 0.0 / PROTEIN: 25.0

# BUFFALO-CHICKEN CELERY SNACK BOX

| PREP TIME: | COOK TIME: | TOTAL TIME: | YIELD: |
|---|---|---|---|
| 15 MINUTES | NONE | 15 MINUTES | 2 SERVINGS |

1 cup leftover shredded rotisserie chicken

2 tablespoons Greek yogurt

2 tablespoons hot sauce (I like Frank's RedHot), or more to taste

1/4 teaspoon garlic powder

1/4 teaspoon onion powder

Kosher salt and freshly ground black pepper, to taste

6 stalks celery, cut in half

1/2 cup strawberries, sliced

1/2 cup grapes

2 tablespoons crumbled blue cheese

1 tablespoon chopped fresh parsley leaves

Here's to the end of wondering what to do with all that leftover chicken from the night before.

Make buffalo chicken! And then stuff it into celery sticks. Because apparently celery is good for you and all that jazz. Yeah: It lowers cholesterol, inflammation, and blood pressure; and it prevents ulcers and protects liver health.

See, lots of good things here! And we use Greek yogurt for extra creaminess without adding too many calories. I kid you not—the entire snack box is 218 calories per serving!

1. Combine the chicken, yogurt, hot sauce, garlic powder, and onion powder in a large bowl; season with salt and pepper to taste. Cover and refrigerate for up to 3 days.

2. Divide the celery sticks, strawberries, and grapes into meal prep containers. The chicken mixture can be kept for 3 days (stored separately) in the refrigerator. The celery boats should be assembled day of serving.

3. To serve, fill the celery stalks with the chicken mixture and top with blue cheese and parsley. Enjoy with the fruit.

**NUTRITION FACTS:** CALORIES: 218.0 / TOTAL FAT: 6.0 / TRANS FAT: 0.0 / SATURATED FAT: 3.0 / CHOLESTEROL: 76.0 / SODIUM: 867.0 / CARBOHYDRATES: 75.0 / FIBER: 3.0 / SUGAR: 11.0 / PROTEIN: 25.0

# CHICKEN AND HUMMUS BISTRO BOX

| PREP TIME: 20 MINUTES | COOK TIME: 10 MINUTES | TOTAL TIME: 30 MINUTES | YIELD: 4 SERVINGS |
|---|---|---|---|

1 pound boneless, skinless chicken breasts, cut into strips

½ teaspoon garlic powder

¼ teaspoon onion powder

Kosher salt and freshly ground black pepper, to taste

1 cucumber, thinly sliced

4 mini whole wheat pitas

1 cup cherry tomatoes

½ cup hummus (homemade or store-bought)

This is another re-creation of a Starbucks menu item. *But,* mine is way better. Sorry, Starbs, but it is. Here's why:

Prepping anything fresh in your own kitchen always ensures a cleaner, less artificially modified, healthier end result. Most prepackaged items in stores have tons of preservatives to increase their shelf life. Not to mention the salt content. If you eat too much salt, it creates an increase in water stored in your body, which raises your blood pressure. So, the more salt you eat, the higher your blood pressure. The higher your blood pressure, the greater the strain on your heart, kidneys, and brain.

So, let's stick with the homemade version. We consume less salt and spend less money! Win for all!

1. Preheat a grill to medium-high heat. Season the chicken with the garlic powder, onion powder, salt, and pepper.

2. Add the chicken to the grill and cook, flipping once, until cooked through and the juices run clear, 5 to 6 minutes on each side; set aside until cool.

3. Divide the chicken, cucumber, pita bread, tomatoes, and hummus into meal prep containers. Refrigerate for up to 3 days.

**NUTRITION FACTS:** CALORIES: 205.0 / TOTAL FAT: 6.0 / TRANS FAT: 0.0 / SATURATED FAT: 1.0 / CHOLESTEROL: 65.0 / SODIUM: 626.0 / CARBOHYDRATES: 16.0 / FIBER: 2.0 / SUGAR: 2.0 / PROTEIN: 22.0

# CHOCOLATE-STRAWBERRY ENERGY BITES

| PREP TIME:<br>20 MINUTES | COOK TIME:<br>1 HOUR | TOTAL TIME:<br>1 HOUR 20 MINUTES | YIELD:<br>5 SERVINGS (15 BITES) |
| --- | --- | --- | --- |

1 cup old-fashioned rolled oats

1/2 cup unsweetened shredded coconut

1/3 cup cashew butter

1/4 cup honey*

3 tablespoons chia seeds

1/2 teaspoon vanilla extract

1/4 teaspoon kosher salt

3/4 cup finely chopped freeze-dried strawberries

1/4 cup mini chocolate chips*

When it comes to snacking, I want something sweet at first. The next minute, I want something salty. Then I need something crunchy yet soft…It's exhausting to make up my mind. So, I created these little bites of heaven to satisfy *any* kind of craving.

I came up with this idea when I was packing for a hike. I needed something to satisfy my sweet tooth, but nothing too heavy. And it obviously needed to be nutritious and easy to transport. My hands are already full enough as it is when Butters decides he doesn't feel like walking anymore and I have to carry him all the way to the bottom.

Fortunately, these bites have complex carbs (oats) for sustained energy, strawberry and chocolate chips for your sweet tooth, and chia seeds for all their nutritional benefits. Yes, these energy bites really have. it. all.

1. Line a baking sheet with waxed paper or parchment paper; set aside.

2. In a food processor, pulse the oats and coconut until the mixture resembles a coarse flour, 5 to 6 pulses; transfer to a medium bowl.

3. Using a wooden spoon, stir in the cashew butter, honey, chia seeds, vanilla, and salt until well combined. Stir in the strawberries and chocolate chips until incorporated.

4. Knead the mixture together and form into 15 (1-inch) balls, about 1 1/2 tablespoons each. Place on the prepared baking sheet in a single layer.

5. Refrigerate until firm, about 1 hour. Store in an airtight container in the refrigerator for up to 1 week, or the freezer for up to 1 month.

**NOTE**
* If you are vegan, you can sub in agave for the honey and cacao nibs for the chocolate chips.

**NUTRITION FACTS:** CALORIES: 342.0 / TOTAL FAT: 16.0 / TRANS FAT: 0.0 / SATURATED FAT: 5.0 / CHOLESTEROL: 0.0 / SODIUM: 250.0 / CARBOHYDRATES: 53.0 / FIBER: 6.0 / SUGAR: 29.0 / PROTEIN: 8.0

# DELI SNACK BOX

| PREP TIME: 15 MINUTES | COOK TIME: 10 MINUTES | TOTAL TIME: 25 MINUTES | YIELD: 1 SERVING |
|---|---|---|---|

1 large egg

1½ ounces thinly sliced turkey breast

¼ cup cherry tomatoes

1 ounce sharp cheddar cheese, cubed

4 pita bites crackers

1 tablespoon raw almonds

The first time I made this snack box, I had forgotten what I'd packed in my cooler. I loaded up the car for a busy day with the usual cargo: my camera, laptop, workout bag, food cooler, and Butters, of course.

I dropped off Butters at daycare, attempted to run 3.5 miles while dancing to *NSYNC, grocery shopped, and made a few returns.

Hours later, I reached into the cargo to find this fun snack box. I inhaled the crackers and cheese first, because, well, hello, that's what gets priority.

After my cheese inhalation, I also got my turkey, a hard-boiled egg, sweet tomatoes, and crunchy almonds—all of it for under 355 calories.

And it kept me going completely until dinnertime. There's just no getting hangry here!

1. Place the egg in a saucepan and cover with cold water by 1 inch. Bring to a boil and cook for 1 minute. Cover the pan with a tight-fitting lid and remove from heat; let sit for 8 to 10 minutes. Drain well and let cool before peeling.

2. Place the turkey, egg, tomatoes, cheese, crackers, and almonds into a meal prep container. This can be kept in the refrigerator for up to 3 days.

**NUTRITION FACTS:** CALORIES: 353.0 / TOTAL FAT: 22.0 / TRANS FAT: 0.0 / SATURATED FAT: 8.0 / CHOLESTEROL: 261.0 / SODIUM: 343.0 / CARBOHYDRATES: 11.0 / FIBER: 1.0 / SUGAR: 1.0 / PROTEIN: 29.0

# DIY PIZZA SNACKABLES

| PREP TIME:<br>10 MINUTES | COOK TIME:<br>NONE | TOTAL TIME:<br>10 MINUTES | YIELD:<br>1 SERVING |
| --- | --- | --- | --- |

4 pita bites crackers

2 tablespoons shredded reduced-fat mozzarella cheese

2 tablespoons pizza sauce

2 tablespoons almonds

1 tablespoon mini pepperoni

¼ cup grapes

I grew up in a very traditional Korean household. That basically means my mom never bought me Lunchables. Never, ever, ever. I would just watch my friends and the other cool kids eating their own Lunchables during lunchtime, and sipping on their Capri Suns. Oh, how I was jealous of their Capri Suns.

But now that I'm 30, I actually just make my own version of Lunchables. You know, because I clearly have a lot of lost time to make up for!

So, here's my spin on the pizza version. And at 275 calories per serving, you can feel good about eating it! And guys, the caloric numbers do not actually include a Capri Sun. Sorry!

1. Place the crackers, cheese, pizza sauce, almonds, pepperoni, and grapes into a meal prep container. Refrigerate for up to 3 days.

**NUTRITION FACTS:** CALORIES: 275.0 / TOTAL FAT: 16.0 / TRANS FAT: 0.0 / SATURATED FAT: 4.0 / CHOLESTEROL: 15.0 / SODIUM: 369.0 / CARBOHYDRATES: 21.0 / FIBER: 2.0 / SUGAR: 9.0 / PROTEIN: 10.0

# GREEK CHICKPEA POWER SALAD

| PREP TIME:<br>20 MINUTES | COOK TIME:<br>NONE | TOTAL TIME:<br>20 MINUTES | YIELD:<br>4 SERVINGS |
|---|---|---|---|

**OREGANO-GARLIC VINAIGRETTE**

¼ cup extra-virgin olive oil

3 tablespoons red wine vinegar

2 teaspoons dried oregano

1½ teaspoons whole grain mustard

1 clove garlic, pressed

¼ teaspoon sugar (optional)

Kosher salt and freshly ground black pepper, to taste

1 (15-ounce) can garbanzo beans, rinsed and drained

1 pint grape tomatoes, halved

1 yellow bell pepper, diced

1 orange bell pepper, diced

2 Persian cucumbers, halved lengthwise and thinly sliced

1 cup chopped fresh parsley leaves

⅓ cup diced red onion

1 (4-ounce) container feta cheese, crumbled

I could snack on this nonstop, whether it's in the middle of my workday or after a Pilates class. Because the last thing I want to do is go grab an old-fashioned donut after working my butt off for 45 minutes. (That's why I eat the donut *before* class.)

But never mind that; let's talk garbanzo beans! These beans (aka chickpeas) are well-known for their nutritious qualities, but did you know that because they are so high in fiber, they are less likely to make you want to snack on other things after you eat them?

Plus, I love feta and I am always looking for new ways to use it. Being a good source of calcium and vitamin A, feta is one of the healthier cheeses. It's also an easy cheese to digest, for those of us who are sensitive to dairy.

So, what did we learn here? Donut first. Pilates second. Chickpea power salad third.

1. FOR THE VINAIGRETTE: In a small bowl, whisk together the olive oil, vinegar, oregano, mustard, garlic, and sugar; season with salt and pepper to taste. Keeps covered in the refrigerator for 3 to 4 days.

2. Combine the garbanzo beans, tomatoes, bell peppers, cucumbers, parsley, onion, and cheese in a large bowl. Divide into meal prep containers. Will keep covered in the refrigerator 3 to 4 days.

3. To serve, pour vinaigrette on the salad and gently toss to combine.

**NUTRITION FACTS:** CALORIES: 305.0 / TOTAL FAT: 20.0 / TRANS FAT: 0.0 / SATURATED FAT: 5.0 / CHOLESTEROL: 17.0 / SODIUM: 480.0 / CARBOHYDRATES: 24.0 / FIBER: 7.0 / SUGAR: 9.0 / PROTEIN: 8.0

# KALE CHIPS SNACK BOX

| PREP TIME: | COOK TIME: | TOTAL TIME: | YIELD: |
|---|---|---|---|
| 20 MINUTES | 1 HOUR | 1 HOUR 20 MINUTES | 4 SERVINGS |

## KALE CHIPS

1 bunch kale, stems and thick ribs removed

2 tablespoons olive oil

1 clove garlic, pressed

Kosher salt and freshly ground black pepper, to taste

## CRISPY GARBANZO BEANS

1 (16-ounce) can garbanzo beans, drained and rinsed

1½ tablespoons olive oil

1½ teaspoons chili lime seasoning

1 cup strawberries, sliced

1 cup grapes

4 tangerines, peeled and segmented*

You'll never believe how easy it is to make kale chips. And it's a great way to get those picky eaters to eat their greens. Plus, kale is a great source of fiber, is low in calories, and has zero fat.

What's great about the chips is that you can season them any way you like. I kept it simple here with garlic, salt, and pepper. But you can add a bit of flair with crushed red pepper flakes or even a sprinkling of paprika. Plus, this pairs so perfectly with the crispy chili lime garbanzo beans!

But I will warn you—please, please, please check your teeth after consumption. Maybe carry some floss with you? Sometimes people don't tell you when you have something stuck in your teeth!

1. Preheat the oven to 375 degrees F. Lightly oil a baking sheet or coat with nonstick spray.

2. FOR THE KALE CHIPS: Place the kale on the prepared baking sheet. Add the olive oil and garlic, and season with salt and pepper. Gently toss to combine and arrange in a single layer. Bake for 10 to 13 minutes, or until crisp; let cool completely. Set aside.

3. FOR THE CRISPY BEANS: Using a clean kitchen towel or paper towels, dry the garbanzo beans thoroughly. Remove and discard skins. Place the garbanzos in a single layer on the baking sheet and bake for 20 minutes. Add the olive oil and chili lime seasoning and gently toss to combine. Bake until crisp and dry, an additional 15 to 17 minutes.

4. Turn off the oven and open the door slightly; cool completely in the oven for 1 hour.

5. Place the strawberries, grapes, and tangerines into meal prep containers. Will keep covered in the refrigerator 3 to 4 days. Kale chips and garbanzos should be kept separately in ziplock bags at room temperature to keep them nice and crisp.

### NOTE
* Tangerines can dry out if not consumed immediately. Keep them unpeeled if meal prepping in advance.

**NUTRITION FACTS:** CALORIES: 308.0 / TOTAL FAT: 16.0 / TRANS FAT: 0.0 / SATURATED FAT: 2.0 / CHOLESTEROL: 0.0 / SODIUM: 292.0 / CARBOHYDRATES: 38.0 / FIBER: 8.0 / SUGAR: 19.0 / PROTEIN: 8.0

# MINI PUMPKIN PROTEIN DONUTS

| PREP TIME:<br>30 MINUTES | COOK TIME:<br>10 MINUTES | TOTAL TIME:<br>40 MINUTES | YIELD:<br>6 SERVINGS (24 DONUTS) |
|---|---|---|---|

1 cup white whole wheat flour

½ cup vanilla whey protein powder

⅓ cup firmly packed light brown sugar

1½ teaspoons baking powder

1 teaspoon pumpkin pie spice

¼ teaspoon kosher salt

1 cup canned pumpkin puree

3 tablespoons unsalted butter, melted

2 large egg whites

2 tablespoons 2% milk

1 teaspoon ground cinnamon

⅓ cup granulated sugar

2 tablespoons unsalted butter, melted

**SPECIAL EQUIPMENT**

Mini-donut pan

There's no better way to welcome fall than with these mini pumpkin donuts.

I have tried to make them as *healthy* as I possibly can. I use whole wheat flour instead of plain, and I even added some whey protein powder to keep my muscles and brain (and trainer) happy.

When I see them packed in my lunch box, I only see four little protein-filled rewards. That is, after I eat my grilled chicken kale salad, which I usually end up inhaling as fast as I can so I can get to the donut part.

I mean, guys, come on: By now you know me so well. DONUTS ARE MY JAM!!! No pun intended. Okay, enough about this. Please go try them for yourself! And remember, it's four donuts per serving!

1. Preheat the oven to 350 degrees F. Coat the cups of the donut pan with nonstick spray.

2. In a large bowl, combine the flour, protein powder, brown sugar, baking powder, pumpkin pie spice, and salt.

3. In a large glass measuring cup or another bowl, whisk together the pumpkin, butter, egg whites, and milk.

4. Pour the wet mixture over the dry ingredients and stir, using a rubber spatula, just until moist.

5. Scoop the batter evenly into the donut pan. Bake for 8 to 10 minutes, until the donuts are lightly browned and spring back when touched. Cool for 5 minutes.

6. Combine the cinnamon and sugar in a small bowl. Dip each donut into the melted butter and then into the cinnamon sugar.

7. Serve warm or at room temperature. Store in an airtight container up to 5 days.

**NUTRITION FACTS:** CALORIES: 319.0 / TOTAL FAT: 10.0 / TRANS FAT: 0.0 / SATURATED FAT: 6.0 / CHOLESTEROL: 43.0 / SODIUM: 468.0 / CARBOHYDRATES: 49.0 / FIBER: 3.0 / SUGAR: 18.0 / PROTEIN: 11.0

# RAINBOW HUMMUS VEGGIE PINWHEELS

| PREP TIME:<br>15 MINUTES | COOK TIME:<br>NONE | TOTAL TIME:<br>15 MINUTES | YIELD:<br>4 SERVINGS |
|---|---|---|---|

2 tablespoons hummus (homemade or store-bought)

1 (8-inch) spinach tortilla

1/4 cup thinly sliced red bell pepper

1/4 cup thinly sliced yellow bell pepper

1/4 cup thinly sliced carrot

1/4 cup thinly sliced cucumber

1/4 cup baby spinach

1/4 cup shredded red cabbage

1/4 cup alfalfa sprouts

1/2 cup strawberries

1/2 cup blueberries

When I was getting my master's in public health, they taught me something I would never forget: We eat with our eyes.

I mean, yes, that's very true with Instagram and all. But really—seeing colorful foods inspires us to eat healthier. And eating a rainbow of foods is a great way to ensure that we are getting a variety of vitamins and minerals, as different antioxidants create the different colors in fruits and vegetables.

The colors in the pinwheels are so incredibly vibrant, which makes for such a fun snack. That is, they're almost a shame to eat. But we really should, especially since we stuffed the crap out of them with hummus.

1. Spread the hummus over the surface of the tortilla in an even layer, leaving a 1/4-inch border. Place the bell peppers, carrot, cucumber, spinach, cabbage, and sprouts in the center of the tortilla. Bring the bottom edge of the tortilla tightly over the vegetables, folding in the sides. Continue rolling until the top of the tortilla is reached. Cut into sixths.

2. Place pinwheels, strawberries, and blueberries into a meal prep container. Refrigerate for 3 to 4 days.

NUTRITION FACTS: CALORIES: 320.0 / TOTAL FAT: 8.0 / TRANS FAT: 0.0 / SATURATED FAT: 2.0 / CHOLESTEROL: 0.0 / SODIUM: 370.0 / CARBOHYDRATES: 59.0 / FIBER: 12.0 / SUGAR: 15.0 / PROTEIN: 8.0

# SALSA SNACK BOX

| PREP TIME:<br>15 MINUTES | COOK TIME:<br>NONE | TOTAL TIME:<br>15 MINUTES | YIELD:<br>4 SERVINGS |
| --- | --- | --- | --- |

¾ cup diced strawberries

¾ cup diced mango

1 jalapeño, seeded and minced

2 tablespoons diced red onion

2 tablespoons chopped fresh cilantro leaves

2 teaspoons honey

Juice of 1 lime

2 cups tortilla chips

1 red bell pepper, thinly sliced

1 orange bell pepper, thinly sliced

1 jicama, peeled and sliced into thick matchsticks

1 pineapple, cut into wedges

Lo and behold—my favorite snack box yet! Well, maybe it's a close second after the Mini Pumpkin Protein Donuts (on page 176). No, but really, snacking has never been so stinking good until now.

The strawberry mango salsa here is perfectly sweet and savory to satisfy any mid-afternoon craving. And the longer it sits, the better it tastes!

Now you can always decrease or increase the amount of jalapeño depending on how much heat you prefer. And please remember to wash your hands immediately after handling a jalapeño pepper. There's nothing worse than hot pepper hands!

1. In a large bowl, combine the strawberries, mango, jalapeño, onion, cilantro, honey, and lime juice.

2. Divide the tortilla chips into ziplock bags. Divide the salsa, bell peppers, jicama, and pineapple into meal prep containers. Will keep in the refrigerator 3 to 4 days.

**NUTRITION FACTS:** CALORIES: 262.0 / TOTAL FAT: 4.0 / TRANS FAT: 0.0 / SATURATED FAT: 1.0 / CHOLESTEROL: 0.0 / SODIUM: 71.0 / CARBOHYDRATES: 55.0 / FIBER: 12.0 / SUGAR: 22.0 / PROTEIN: 1.0

# TUNA SALAD MEAL PREP

| PREP TIME:<br>15 MINUTES | COOK TIME:<br>10 MINUTES | TOTAL TIME:<br>25 MINUTES | YIELD:<br>4 SERVINGS |
|---|---|---|---|

2 large eggs

2 (5-ounce) cans tuna in water, drained and flaked

1/2 cup nonfat Greek yogurt

1/4 cup diced celery

1/4 cup diced red onion

1 tablespoon Dijon mustard

1 tablespoon sweet pickle relish (optional)

1 teaspoon freshly squeezed lemon juice, or more to taste

1/4 teaspoon garlic powder

Kosher salt and freshly ground black pepper, to taste

4 Bibb lettuce leaves*

1/2 cup raw almonds

1 cucumber, sliced

1 apple (I like Braeburn), sliced**

This high-protein snack box has a secret ingredient. Well, two secret ingredients—Greek yogurt and Dijon mustard. They make the perfect alternative to mayonnaise, and you won't miss the mayo at all. I promise.

The tuna is naturally high in protein. Perhaps the most common health benefit that is attributed to tuna fish is its significant impact on heart health. It has very high levels of omega-3 fatty acids, which help to reduce omega-6 fatty acids and cholesterol in the arteries and blood vessels.

So, basically, I'm providing you guys with happy, healthy hearts!

1. Place the eggs in a large saucepan and cover with cold water by 1 inch. Bring to a boil and cook for 1 minute. Cover the pot with a tight-fitting lid and remove from the heat; let sit for 8 to 10 minutes. Drain well and let cool before peeling and halving.

2. In a medium bowl, combine the tuna, yogurt, celery, onion, mustard, relish, lemon juice, and garlic powder; season with salt and pepper to taste.

3. Divide lettuce leaves into meal prep containers. Top with tuna mixture, and add the eggs, almonds, cucumber, and apple to the side. Will keep in the refrigerator 3 to 4 days.

**NOTES**

* I use the lettuce cup as a moisture barrier, keeping all of my compartments aligned and separate. It's not really meant for consumption. However, if you prefer a tuna salad lettuce wrap, just be sure to pack your lettuce leaves in a separate ziplock bag to avoid sogginess!

** A squeeze of lemon juice on the apple slices should keep them from browning.

**NUTRITION FACTS:** CALORIES: 186.0 / TOTAL FAT: 8.0 / TRANS FAT: 0.0 / SATURATED FAT: 1.0 / CHOLESTEROL: 113.0 / SODIUM: 422.0 / CARBOHYDRATES: 11.0 / FIBER: 2.0 / SUGAR: 5.0 / PROTEIN: 18.0

TURKEY AND
VEGGIE LASAGNA

# 9. Freezer Meals

# BUTTERNUT SQUASH FRITTERS

| PREP TIME:<br>20 MINUTES | COOK TIME:<br>20 MINUTES | TOTAL TIME:<br>40 MINUTES | YIELD:<br>MAKES 25 FRITTERS |
|---|---|---|---|

4 cups shredded butternut squash

⅓ cup white whole wheat flour

2 cloves garlic, minced

2 large eggs, beaten

½ teaspoon dried thyme

¼ teaspoon dried sage

Pinch of nutmeg

Kosher salt and freshly ground black pepper, to taste

2 tablespoons olive oil

¼ cup Greek yogurt (optional)

2 tablespoons chopped fresh chives (optional)

This is what fall is all about.

The smells of rich, warm sage and thyme just filling up the house as I cozy up in front of the fireplace…Except, in reality, it's 103 degrees in Los Angeles at the end of October.

I wish I were joking. Ben and I took his parents to Game 1 of the Dodgers' World Series in October last year. And it was 106 degrees.

But let's focus on the good stuff instead: These bad boys are like a healthier version of a potato latke, with only 149 calories in a single serving!

You can also enjoy the fritters for breakfast topped with eggs, and maybe some bacon if you're feeling really indulgent!

1. In a large bowl, combine the squash, flour, garlic, eggs, thyme, sage, and nutmeg; season with salt and pepper.

2. Heat the olive oil in a large skillet over medium-high heat. In batches, scoop about 2 tablespoons of batter for each fritter, add to the pan, and flatten with a spatula. Cook until the undersides are nicely golden brown, about 2 minutes. Flip and cook on the other side, 1 to 2 minutes longer. Transfer to a paper towel–lined plate.

3. Serve immediately, with Greek yogurt and chives if desired.

4. TO FREEZE: Place the cooked fritters on a baking sheet in a single layer; cover tightly with plastic wrap, and freeze overnight. Transfer to freezer bags and store in the freezer for up to 3 months. When ready to serve, bake at 350 degrees F for about 10 to 15 minutes, until warmed, flipping halfway. Transfer to a paper towel–lined plate.

**NUTRITION FACTS:** CALORIES: 149.0 / TOTAL FAT: 7.0 / TRANS FAT: 0.0 / SATURATED FAT: 1.0 / CHOLESTEROL: 62.0 / SODIUM: 30.0 / CARBOHYDRATES: 17.0 / FIBER: 2.0 / SUGAR: 2.0 / PROTEIN: 5.0

# CARROT GINGER SOUP

| PREP TIME: 20 MINUTES | COOK TIME: 35 MINUTES | TOTAL TIME: 55 MINUTES | YIELD: 6 SERVINGS (10 CUPS) |
|---|---|---|---|

2 pounds carrots, peeled and chopped*

1 sweet potato (about 8 ounces), peeled and chopped

1 sweet onion, chopped

3 cloves garlic

1 (¾-inch) piece fresh ginger, peeled and sliced

1 teaspoon smoked paprika

2 bay leaves

6 cups vegetable stock, plus more if needed

Kosher salt and freshly ground black pepper, to taste

⅓ cup fresh cilantro leaves

¼ cup fresh mint leaves

2 tablespoons freshly squeezed lime juice

⅓ cup heavy cream

¼ teaspoon smoked paprika (optional)

I remember constantly being told to eat my carrots because they were good for my eyes. I also remember feeling like my eyesight didn't seem any stronger after I ate them. I guess I was hoping for X-ray vision or something?

But since then, I have learned that carrots really are beneficial to our health. They're high in vitamin A, which is actually much-needed for healthy eyes as well as a healthy immune system. They are also a nice source of fiber.

On top of the carrots, this soup is full of ingredients that will make you feel so good. Ginger is known for helping during illness, is great for digestion, and is a natural remedy for stomachaches.

While you might not be able to see through walls, you definitely will do your body good here.

1. Combine the carrots, sweet potato, onion, garlic, ginger, paprika, bay leaves, and stock in a large Dutch oven; season with salt and pepper.

2. Bring to a boil; reduce the heat and simmer until the carrots are tender, 25 to 30 minutes. Stir in the cilantro, mint, and lime juice. Discard the bay leaves.

3. Puree with an immersion blender to desired consistency. If the soup is too thick, add more stock as needed.

4. Stir in the cream and cook until heated through, about 2 minutes. Serve immediately, garnished with paprika if desired.

5. TO FREEZE: Omit the cream until ready to serve. Portion the cooled soup into ziplock freezer bags and lay the bags flat in a single layer in the freezer. To serve, add the cream and reheat over low heat, stirring occasionally, until heated through.

**NOTE**
* Baby carrots can be substituted for the chopped carrots.

**NUTRITION FACTS:** CALORIES: 131.0 / TOTAL FAT: 6.0 / TRANS FAT: 0.0 / SATURATED FAT: 3.0 / CHOLESTEROL: 19.0 / SODIUM: 974.0 / CARBOHYDRATES: 17.0 / FIBER: 2.0 / SUGAR: 7.0 / PROTEIN: 2.0

# CHEESY CHICKEN AND BROCCOLI RICE CASSEROLE

| PREP TIME: 15 MINUTES | COOK TIME: 45 MINUTES | TOTAL TIME: 1 HOUR | YIELD: 6 SERVINGS |
|---|---|---|---|

1 (6-ounce) package long-grain and wild rice mix

3 tablespoons unsalted butter

3 cloves garlic, minced

1 onion, diced

2 cups cremini mushrooms, quartered

1 stalk celery, diced

½ teaspoon dried thyme

1 tablespoon all-purpose flour

¼ cup dry white wine

1¼ cups chicken stock

Kosher salt and freshly ground black pepper, to taste

3 cups broccoli florets

½ cup sour cream

2 cups leftover shredded rotisserie chicken

1 cup shredded reduced-fat cheddar cheese, divided

2 tablespoons chopped fresh parsley leaves (optional)

Some nights, you just want to stay in and eat something warm and comforting. (Wait. I think that's *all* nights for me. With a 7:25 p.m. bedtime.) Well, that's exactly what this casserole serves to do. It has all the same components of your mom's classic casserole, except it's healthier!

We're using reduced-fat cheddar cheese here but don't worry: I didn't omit the sour cream. Sometimes you just need the good stuff. And you know what? One serving is still less than 500 calories.

1. Preheat the oven to 375 degrees F.

2. Cook the rice mix according to package instructions; set aside.

3. Melt the butter in a large ovenproof skillet over medium-high heat. Add the garlic, onion, mushrooms, and celery and cook, stirring occasionally, until tender, 3 to 4 minutes. Stir in the thyme and cook until fragrant, about 1 minute.

4. Whisk in the flour until lightly browned, about 1 minute. Gradually whisk in the wine and stock. Cook, whisking constantly, until slightly thickened, 2 to 3 minutes; season with salt and pepper to taste.

5. Stir in the broccoli, sour cream, chicken, ½ cup of the cheese, and the rice. If freezing the casserole for later use, stop here and skip to step 7. Otherwise, sprinkle with the remaining ½ cup cheese.

6. Transfer the skillet to the oven and bake until the casserole is bubbly and heated through, 20 to 22 minutes. Serve immediately, garnished with parsley if desired.

7. TO FREEZE: Transfer the unbaked casserole mixture to a ziplock freezer bag and lay the bag flat in the freezer. Freeze for up to 3 months. When ready to serve, thaw overnight in the refrigerator. To reheat, transfer to an ovenproof skillet or baking pan, sprinkle with ½ cup cheddar cheese, and bake at 375 degrees F for 20 to 30 minutes, until heated through.

**NUTRITION FACTS:** CALORIES: 448.0 / TOTAL FAT: 23.0 / TRANS FAT: 0.0 / SATURATED FAT: 11.0 / CHOLESTEROL: 144.0 / SODIUM: 897.0 / CARBOHYDRATES: 27.0 / FIBER: 2.0 / SUGAR: 4.0 / PROTEIN: 28.0

# CHICKEN AND QUINOA TORTILLA SOUP

| PREP TIME: 15 MINUTES | COOK TIME: 45 MINUTES | TOTAL TIME: 1 HOUR | YIELD: 8 SERVINGS (12 CUPS) |
|---|---|---|---|

### BAKED TORTILLA STRIPS

4 corn tortillas, cut into thin strips

½ teaspoon chili powder, or more to taste

Kosher salt and freshly ground black pepper, to taste

1 tablespoon olive oil

1 pound boneless, skinless chicken breasts

Kosher salt and freshly ground black pepper, to taste

3 cloves garlic, minced

1 onion, diced

1 green bell pepper, diced

2 tablespoons tomato paste

1 tablespoon chili powder

1½ teaspoons ground cumin

1 teaspoon dried oregano

8 cups chicken stock

1 (28-ounce) can diced tomatoes

1 (15-ounce) can black beans, drained and rinsed

1½ cups corn kernels (frozen, canned, or roasted)

*(continued)*

I went to Indianapolis for the first time during the holidays. I remember distinctly just how cold it was. It was literally around 5 degrees F. My legs were ice because I'm the girl who wore jeans in 5-degree weather. I'm also the girl who lives in LA and doesn't know any better.

But we walked into this really fun Mexican restaurant, and while Ben ordered enchiladas, I ordered the chicken tortilla soup. I don't know if it was the cold or if it was just that good, but this soup was *life*. Just *life*. I took that first spoonful and just yelled out, "Ooooooooh…"—similar to how Joey says it when he eats a meatball sub.

So, I came home and tried to re-create it, except I think my version is a little better. Not to toot my own horn—but guys, a single serving has less than 300 calories and that includes the homemade baked tortilla strips! Plus, the quinoa brings in more protein and fiber.

1. FOR THE TORTILLA STRIPS: Preheat the oven to 375 degrees F. Lightly oil a baking sheet or coat with nonstick spray.

2. Spread the tortilla strips in a single layer on the prepared baking sheet; season with the chili powder, salt, and pepper and coat with nonstick spray. Bake until crisp and golden, 10 to 12 minutes, stirring halfway; set aside and let cool.

3. Heat the olive oil in a large stockpot or Dutch oven over medium heat. Season the chicken with salt and pepper. Add the chicken to the pot and cook until golden, 2 to 3 minutes per side; transfer to a plate and set aside.

4. Add the garlic, onion, and bell pepper to the pot and cook, stirring occasionally, until tender, 3 to 4 minutes. Stir in the tomato paste, chili powder, cumin, and oregano and cook until fragrant, about 1 minute. Stir in the chicken, along with the stock, tomatoes, black beans, and corn. Bring to a boil; reduce

*(continued)*

**NUTRITION FACTS:** CALORIES: 281.0 / TOTAL FAT: 6.0 / TRANS FAT: 0.0 / SATURATED FAT: 1.0 / CHOLESTEROL: 54.0 / SODIUM: 1439.0 / CARBOHYDRATES: 28.0 / FIBER: 5.0 / SUGAR: 3.0 / PROTEIN: 22.0

½ cup quinoa

Juice of 1 lime

½ cup chopped fresh cilantro leaves

Optional garnishes: shredded cheddar cheese, minced red onion, jalapeño slices, cilantro leaves

the heat and simmer, uncovered, until the chicken is tender and cooked through, 20 to 25 minutes. Remove the chicken from the pot and shred, using two forks.

5. Return the shredded chicken to the pot along with the quinoa and simmer, uncovered, until the quinoa is tender, 15 to 20 minutes. Stir in the lime juice and cilantro and season with salt and pepper to taste.

6. Serve immediately with the baked tortilla strips, and additional garnishes if desired.

7. TO FREEZE: Omit the tortilla strips and garnishes until ready to serve. Portion the cooled soup into ziplock freezer bags and lay the bags flat in a single layer in the freezer. Reheat the soup over low heat, stirring occasionally, until heated through.

# TURKEY TAMALE PIES WITH CORNBREAD CRUST

| PREP TIME:<br>30 MINUTES | COOK TIME:<br>35 MINUTES | TOTAL TIME:<br>1 HOUR 5 MINUTES | YIELD:<br>6 SERVINGS |
|---|---|---|---|

## FILLING

1 tablespoon olive oil

1 pound ground turkey breast

2 cloves garlic, minced

1 onion, diced

1 medium poblano pepper, seeded and diced

2 teaspoons chili powder

1 teaspoon dried oregano

¾ teaspoon ground cumin

Kosher salt and freshly ground black pepper, to taste

2 (14.5-ounce) cans Mexican-style stewed tomatoes

1 cup corn kernels (frozen, canned, or roasted)

2 tablespoons chopped fresh cilantro leaves, plus more for garnish

*(continued)*

Whenever a friend or colleague visits me in Los Angeles, they all ask for the same thing: Mexican food. Southern California has, of course, incredible Mexican food, so it's a no-brainer that this is a top choice for everyone.

I mean, hello, have you had Tacos Por Favor? It's a popular Mexican chain restaurant, usually in a strip mall, with the best chicken tamale plate in the entire world. Or at least in all of Los Angeles.

I took their most popular offering and came up with this recipe for individual tamale pies (for easy serving and portion control, of course), using turkey instead of chicken and topping it off with the most epic cornbread crust.

The filling can be stored in the freezer for up to 3 months, but the crust must be made the day it is served. But don't worry. It will take just 5 minutes to whip up! No mixer, no fuss here.

---

1. Preheat the oven to 425 degrees F. Lightly oil 6 (10-ounce) ramekins or coat with nonstick spray.

2. FOR THE FILLING: Heat the olive oil in a large skillet over medium-high heat. Add the ground turkey, garlic, onion, and poblano. Cook until the turkey has browned, 3 to 5 minutes, making sure to crumble the turkey as it cooks. Stir in the chili powder, oregano, and cumin; season with salt and pepper. Drain excess fat.

3. Stir in the tomatoes and break them up with the back of a spoon. Bring to a simmer and stir in the corn and cilantro. Divide the mixture into the prepared ramekins.

4. FOR THE CRUST: Combine the cornmeal, flour, baking powder, and salt in a medium bowl. In a large glass measuring cup or another bowl, whisk together the buttermilk, egg, and butter. Pour the wet mixture over the dry ingredients and stir, using a rubber spatula, just until moist. Add the cheese and cilantro, and gently toss to combine.

*(continued)*

**NUTRITION FACTS:** CALORIES: 312.0 / TOTAL FAT: 12.0 / TRANS FAT: 0.0 / SATURATED FAT: 5.0 / CHOLESTEROL: 46.0 / SODIUM: 859.0 / CARBOHYDRATES: 30.0 / FIBER: 2.0 / SUGAR: 6.0 / PROTEIN: 20.0

**CHEDDAR-CILANTRO CORNBREAD CRUST**

½ cup yellow cornmeal

¼ cup all-purpose flour

1 teaspoon baking powder

¼ teaspoon kosher salt

¾ cup low-fat buttermilk

1 large egg

1 tablespoon unsalted butter, melted

¾ cup shredded extra-sharp cheddar cheese

¼ cup chopped fresh cilantro leaves

5. Top the filling in the ramekins with the crust mixture in an even layer. Place on a baking sheet and bake until golden brown and the crust is set, about 25 minutes. Let cool 10 minutes before serving, garnished with additional cilantro leaves.

6. TO FREEZE: Don't make the crust until the day of serving. Prepare the filling to the end of step 3, then cover the individual ramekins tightly with plastic wrap. Freeze for up to 3 months. To serve, remove the plastic wrap. Cover the ramekins with aluminum foil and bake at 425 degrees F for 45 minutes while you make the crust. Uncover the ramekins and top with the crust mixture. Bake for an additional 20 to 30 minutes, until completely cooked through.

# DETOX CHICKEN SOUP

| PREP TIME: | COOK TIME: | TOTAL TIME: | YIELD: |
|------------|------------|-------------|--------|
| 10 MINUTES | 25 MINUTES | 35 MINUTES | 6 SERVINGS |

2 tablespoons olive oil, divided

1 pound boneless, skinless chicken breasts, cut into 1-inch chunks

Kosher salt and freshly ground black pepper, to taste

1 onion, diced

2 carrots, peeled and diced

2 stalks celery, diced

4 cloves garlic, minced

16 ounces cremini mushrooms, thinly sliced

½ teaspoon dried thyme

½ teaspoon dried oregano

8 cups chicken stock

2 bay leaves

½ cup whole wheat orzo pasta

1 sprig fresh rosemary

1 bunch kale, stems removed and leaves chopped

1 (15-ounce) can cannellini beans, drained and rinsed

Juice of 1 lemon

2 tablespoons chopped fresh parsley leaves

I don't know about you guys, but after the holiday season, I feel like someone could literally just roll me around to get from point A to point B. I have eaten so much that I can actually feel my body begging for a break. But this detox soup is the perfect meal for when you want to shake off the holidays and begin again with a clean slate. It's basically better than juicing.

For starters, the cremini mushrooms here are known for their anti-inflammatory and antioxidant properties. They also contain B vitamins, which are essential for good health.

Kale is a superfood containing vitamins A, C, and K. It is also a good source of iron.

Cannellini beans are high in protein and fiber, benefiting your heart and skin.

Lemons are chock-full of beneficial elements. There is a reason drinking lemon water is so highly recommended. It's because lemons have vitamins A, C, E, and $B_6$, as well as potassium, iron, and zinc.

The herbs not only add an amazing amount of flavor but they all provide health benefits as well: Rosemary is antibacterial, thyme has high levels of vitamin C that boosts immunity, bay leaves soothe body aches, and oregano helps detoxify the body.

This soup is so full of nutrients and antioxidants that it's a perfect meal during the dreaded cold and flu season. So, go ahead and store it in the freezer for up to 3 months. You will be beyond relieved and happy when that cold creeps up on you and you have this soup already made.

1. Heat 1 tablespoon of the olive oil in a large stockpot or Dutch oven over medium heat. Season the chicken with salt and pepper. Add the chicken to the stockpot and cook until golden, 2 to 3 minutes; transfer the chicken to a plate and set aside.

*(continued)*

**NUTRITION FACTS:** CALORIES: 403.0 / TOTAL FAT: 7.0 / TRANS FAT: 0.0 / SATURATED FAT: 1.0 / CHOLESTEROL: 54.0 / SODIUM: 1635.0 / CARBOHYDRATES: 50.0 / FIBER: 7.0 / SUGAR: 1.0 / PROTEIN: 31.0

2. Add the remaining 1 tablespoon oil to the pot. Add the onion, carrots, and celery and cook, stirring occasionally, until tender, 3 to 4 minutes. Add the garlic and mushrooms and cook, stirring occasionally, until tender and browned, 5 to 6 minutes. Stir in the thyme and oregano and cook until fragrant, about 1 minute.

3. Whisk in the stock and bay leaves; bring to a boil. Stir in the chicken, orzo, and rosemary; reduce the heat and simmer until the orzo is tender, 10 to 12 minutes.

4. Stir in the kale and beans and cook until the kale has wilted, 3 to 4 minutes. Stir in the lemon juice and parsley and season with salt and pepper to taste. Remove the bay leaves and rosemary stem before portioning. Serve immediately.

5. TO FREEZE: Don't add the orzo in step 3. (This is because the pasta can taste a bit mushy upon reheating.) Portion the cooled soup into ziplock freezer bags and lay the bags flat in a single layer in the freezer. When ready to serve, cook the orzo in a large pot of boiling water. Reheat the soup over low heat, stirring occasionally, until heated through. Drain the pasta, add to the soup, and serve.

# LENTIL DETOX SOUP

| PREP TIME: 20 MINUTES | COOK TIME: 25 MINUTES | TOTAL TIME: 45 MINUTES | YIELD: 6 SERVINGS (10 CUPS) |
| --- | --- | --- | --- |

1 tablespoon olive oil

1 sweet onion, diced

2 cloves garlic, minced

1 small jalapeño, seeded and diced

1 tablespoon freshly grated ginger

1½ teaspoons Moroccan spice blend

1 teaspoon ground turmeric

½ teaspoon ground cumin

1 pound dried red lentils (about 2 cups)

Kosher salt and freshly ground black pepper, to taste

1½ cups halved grape tomatoes

4 cups baby spinach

¼ cup fresh cilantro leaves

2 tablespoons freshly squeezed lemon juice

½ cup 2% Greek yogurt (optional)

Contrary to popular belief, "detox" doesn't mean you don't get to eat. So don't panic when you see the word *detox* in a recipe. It also doesn't mean we're having a flavorless soup with a bland broth. Would I ever do that to you? Never.

See, lentils are the best when you are trying to watch what you put into your body. You don't need to eat a lot to feel satisfied, plus they are easy on the wallet, making them a perfect budget-friendly substitute for meat. They are also high in fiber, making them great for your digestion, and a healthy source of protein and iron.

While the lentils are the heart of this soup, the seasoning is the real personality here. The Moroccan spice blend, which contains spices such as cinnamon, coriander, and cayenne, packs a flavorful punch.

Turmeric is a spice that has been used for literally thousands of years, and within the last few years it has been rising up through the wellness population. It is an anti-inflammatory that more and more people are using to combat certain ailments, and its anti-oxidants help protect the body from free radicals.

Cumin is another spice that not only adds a ton of flavor but brings in a ton of health benefits as well. It boosts the immune system and is a great source of iron and vitamin C.

1. Heat the olive oil in a large stockpot or Dutch oven over medium heat. Add the onion and cook, stirring frequently, until translucent, 3 to 4 minutes. Stir in the garlic, jalapeño, ginger, spice blend, turmeric, and cumin and cook until fragrant, 1 to 2 minutes.

2. Stir in the lentils and 7½ cups water; season with salt and pepper. Bring to a boil. Cover, reduce the heat, and simmer, stirring occasionally, until the lentils are tender, about 15 minutes.

*(continued)*

NUTRITION FACTS:  CALORIES: 273.0 / TOTAL FAT: 4.0 / TRANS FAT: 0.0 / SATURATED FAT: 0.0 / CHOLESTEROL: 2.0 / SODIUM: 182.0 / CARBOHYDRATES: 43.0 / FIBER: 15.0 / SUGAR: 3.0 / PROTEIN: 20.0

3. Stir in the tomatoes and cook, stirring occasionally, until softened, 5 to 7 minutes. If the mixture is too thick, add more water as needed until desired consistency is reached.

4. Stir in the spinach, cilantro, and lemon juice and cook until the spinach has wilted, 1 to 2 minutes; season with salt and pepper to taste.

5. Serve immediately, garnished with yogurt, if desired.

6. TO FREEZE: Omit the yogurt until ready to serve. Portion the cooled soup into ziplock freezer bags and lay the bags flat in a single layer in the freezer. Reheat over low heat, stirring occasionally, until heated through.

# FLAKY MILE-HIGH WHOLE WHEAT BISCUITS

| PREP TIME: | COOK TIME: | TOTAL TIME: | YIELD: |
|---|---|---|---|
| 45 MINUTES | 15 MINUTES | 1 HOUR | 12 BISCUITS |

2 cups all-purpose flour

2 cups whole wheat pastry flour

4 teaspoons baking powder

1 teaspoon baking soda

1½ teaspoons kosher salt

⅓ cup (⅔ stick) unsalted butter, frozen

1¾ cups buttermilk

This is a healthier twist on the popular biscuits from the blog, because we're using less butter, subbing in some whole wheat pastry flour, and saving on a ton of calories. But don't worry—you won't be able to taste the difference.

The biscuit dough can keep in the freezer for up to 3 months, but once you bake them, it won't be easy to resist eating one straight from the oven!

They are incredible with some jam and butter, or just as a side to a meal like my Fried Chicken TV Dinner on page 266.

1. In a large bowl, combine the flours, baking powder, baking soda, and salt. Grate the butter on the large holes of a box grater and stir into the flour mixture. Add the buttermilk and stir, using a rubber spatula, until a soft dough forms.

2. Working on a lightly floured surface, knead the dough 3 or 4 times, until it comes together. Using a rolling pin, roll the dough into a 1¼-inch-thick rectangle. Cut out 12 rounds using a 2-inch biscuit or cookie cutter.

3. Line a baking sheet with parchment paper or a silicone baking mat. Place the biscuits on the baking sheet and put in the freezer for 15 minutes.*

4. Preheat the oven to 450 degrees F.

5. Transfer the biscuits from the freezer to the oven and bake for 14 to 18 minutes, until golden brown. Serve warm.

6. TO FREEZE: After placing the biscuits on the baking sheet in step 3, cover tightly with plastic wrap, then freeze overnight. Transfer the biscuits to freezer bags and keep in the freezer for up to 3 months. When ready to serve, continue with step 4 with the desired number of biscuits, but bake the frozen biscuits for an additional 5 minutes, or longer as needed.

NOTE
* Popping the biscuits into the freezer helps keep the butter super cold, so when they bake they will rise and puff up even better. Handling the dough warms the butter up, so this is a quick fix.

**NUTRITION FACTS:** CALORIES: 224.0 / TOTAL FAT: 7.0 / TRANS FAT: 0.0 / SATURATED FAT: 4.0 / CHOLESTEROL: 13.0 / SODIUM: 415.0 / CARBOHYDRATES: 35.0 / FIBER: 3.0 / SUGAR: 1.0 / PROTEIN: 6.0

# FREEZER PIZZA DOUGH

| PREP TIME: 1 HOUR | COOK TIME: NONE | TOTAL TIME: 1 HOUR | YIELD: MAKES ENOUGH DOUGH FOR 4 PIZZAS |
|---|---|---|---|

3 cups warm water (105 to 110 degrees F)

2 (¼-ounce) packages fast-rising yeast

2 tablespoons honey

2½ cups white whole wheat flour

1 tablespoon kosher salt

3 tablespoons olive oil

5 cups all-purpose flour, plus more as needed

Having freezer pizza dough in your back pocket is the best. It's like finding a random $5 bill in your jeans.

Sure, you can buy pizza dough at the grocery store, but guys, the homemade version always delivers. The dough is super easy to work with, and you can make four pizzas with this simple recipe, so this will basically cover you for a month's worth of Pizza Fridays.

Not to mention, the crust of each slice of pizza has only 159 calories. That means you have more room to play with your toppings. My all-time favorite combination has to be meatballs and ricotta cheese. It's absolutely killer.

1. Combine the water, yeast, and honey in a small bowl; let stand until foamy, 3 to 5 minutes.

2. In the bowl of an electric mixer fitted with a dough attachment, beat the yeast mixture, whole wheat flour, salt and olive oil at medium speed until well combined.

3. Gradually add the all-purpose flour, ½ cup at a time, until a soft, smooth ball of dough is formed. It should feel elastic and slightly tacky to the touch. Increase the speed to medium-high and beat for 5 minutes.

4. Lightly oil a large bowl or coat with nonstick spray; place the dough in the bowl, turning to coat. Cover with a clean dishtowel and let stand at room temperature until the dough has doubled in size, 30 to 45 minutes.

5. Working on a lightly floured surface, divide the dough into 4 equal pieces. Roll each into a ball and place into separate ziplock bags. Freeze for up to 2 months.

6. When ready to cook, let the dough stand at room temperature until thawed, 4 to 6 hours.

**NUTRITION FACTS (WHOLE RECIPE):** CALORIES: 956.0 / TOTAL FAT: 12.0 / TRANS FAT: 0.0 / SATURATED FAT: 1.0 / CHOLESTEROL: 0.0 / SODIUM: 588.0 / CARBOHYDRATES: 183.0 / FIBER: 12.0 / SUGAR: 9.0 / PROTEIN: 27.0

# GREEK TURKEY MEATBALLS

| PREP TIME:<br>20 MINUTES | COOK TIME:<br>20 MINUTES | TOTAL TIME:<br>40 MINUTES | YIELD:<br>MAKES 20 MEATBALLS<br>(1 SERVING = 6 MEATBALLS) |
|---|---|---|---|

## TZATZIKI SAUCE

1 cup Greek yogurt

1 English cucumber, finely diced

2 cloves garlic, pressed

1 tablespoon chopped fresh dill

1 teaspoon grated lemon zest

1 tablespoon freshly squeezed lemon juice

1 teaspoon chopped fresh mint (optional)

Kosher salt and freshly ground black pepper, to taste

2 tablespoons olive oil

## MEATBALLS

1 pound ground turkey

$1/3$ cup Italian breadcrumbs

$1/4$ cup diced red onion

2 large egg yolks

3 cloves garlic, minced

Grated zest of 1 lemon, plus optional zest strips for garnish

1 teaspoon dried oregano

$1/2$ teaspoon ground cumin

Kosher salt and freshly ground black pepper, to taste

Chopped fresh dill (optional)

Whenever I cook for a potluck, Greek meatballs are my go-to dish. They check off a lot of boxes: They can be made ahead of time. They travel well. And they're always such a hit, because everyone loves a good meatball.

What I love about these meatballs is that they are not as heavy as your typical Italian meatball. The ground turkey gives them a much lighter feel. And the addition of cumin is so much fun. The tzatziki sauce, though—it's my favorite! I could swim in that. And it's made with Greek yogurt. So hello, guilt-free saucing, guys.

Now remember, the key to a flavorful sauce is making sure you refrigerate it for at least 10 minutes so the flavors can really blend. And if you are taking these to a party, wait until you arrive before you drizzle on the sauce.

1. FOR THE TZATZIKI SAUCE: Combine the yogurt, cucumber, garlic, dill, lemon zest and juice, and mint (if using) in a small bowl; season with salt and pepper to taste. Drizzle with the olive oil. Cover and refrigerate for at least 10 minutes, allowing the flavors to meld.

2. FOR THE MEATBALLS: Preheat the oven to 400 degrees F. Lightly oil a 9x13-inch baking dish or coat with nonstick spray.

3. In a large bowl, combine the ground turkey, breadcrumbs, onion, egg yolks, garlic, lemon zest, oregano, cumin, and salt and pepper. Using a wooden spoon or clean hands, stir until well combined. Roll the mixture into 20 meatballs, each $1/4$ to $1/2$ inches in diameter.

4. Place the meatballs in the prepared baking dish and bake for 18 to 20 minutes, until browned all over and cooked through. Serve immediately with the tzatziki sauce, garnished with dill and lemon zest, if desired.

*(continued)*

NUTRITION FACTS: CALORIES: 454.0 / TOTAL FAT: 26.0 / TRANS FAT: 0.0 / SATURATED FAT: 7.0 / CHOLESTEROL: 136.0 / SODIUM: 927.0 / CARBOHYDRATES: 15.0 / FIBER: 0.0 / SUGAR: 4.0 / PROTEIN: 35.0

5. TO FREEZE: Let the baked meatballs cool completely. Place on a baking sheet lined with parchment paper and cover tightly with plastic wrap. Freeze for 1 to 2 hours, until hard. Transfer the meatballs to freezer bags and keep in the freezer for up to 3 months. To serve, thaw overnight in the refrigerator. Bake at 350 degrees F for 15 to 25 minutes, until heated through.

# GREEN BROCCOLI DETOX SOUP

| PREP TIME: 15 MINUTES | COOK TIME: 20 MINUTES | TOTAL TIME: 35 MINUTES | YIELD: 4 SERVINGS (8 CUPS) |
| --- | --- | --- | --- |

1 tablespoon olive oil

1 small fennel bulb, cored and chopped

1 medium sweet onion, chopped

3 cloves garlic, minced

4 cups chicken stock

4 cups finely chopped broccoli

Kosher salt and freshly ground black pepper, to taste

1 (5-ounce) package baby spinach

3 cups lightly packed watercress, plus more for serving

½ cup fresh parsley leaves

¼ cup 2% Greek yogurt

¼ cup chopped roasted almonds

1 tablespoon lemon zest (optional)

The winter months are for soups, stews, and pot roast, so I sometimes feel like it's hard to get your daily dose of green veggies during those cold months. Not that it ever gets that cold in Los Angeles. But this broccoli detox soup is still the perfect solution to get in all your greens during the cold days.

In addition to the broccoli and its multitude of benefits, we have fennel, and it is a double whammy of goodness. It smells and tastes amazing, and contains both vitamins A and C, which are known as strong antioxidants. It is also rich in potassium and helps maintain healthy muscles, nerves, and kidney function.

There's also watercress. A lot of people don't realize just how great it is. It is full of vitamins A, $B_6$, and $B_{12}$. And it has more vitamin C than an orange. Plus, it's known for being an effective cancer fighter.

So, make yourself a batch of broccoli soup, curl up on the couch, stream your favorite binge TV show (like *This Is Us,* with a box of tissues), and savor this warm, healthy bowl of comfort.

---

1. Heat the olive oil in a large stockpot or Dutch oven over medium heat. Add the fennel and onion and cook, stirring occasionally, until golden and tender, 4 to 5 minutes. Stir in the garlic and cook until fragrant, about 1 minute.

2. Stir in the stock and broccoli and season with salt and pepper. Bring to a boil; reduce the heat and simmer until the broccoli is tender, 5 to 7 minutes. Stir in the spinach, watercress, and parsley, and cook until the spinach has wilted, 1 to 2 minutes.

3. Puree with an immersion blender until the desired consistency is reached.

*(continued)*

**NUTRITION FACTS:** CALORIES: 183.0 / TOTAL FAT: 9.0 / TRANS FAT: 0.0 / SATURATED FAT: 0.0 / CHOLESTEROL: 0.0 / SODIUM: 1128.0 / CARBOHYDRATES: 19.0 / FIBER: 5.0 / SUGAR: 5.0 / PROTEIN: 9.0

4. Serve immediately with yogurt, additional watercress, almonds, and lemon zest, if desired.

5. TO FREEZE: Omit the yogurt, watercress, almonds, and lemon zest until ready to serve. Portion the cooled soup into ziplock freezer bags and lay the bags flat in a single layer in the freezer. Reheat over low heat, stirring occasionally, until heated through.

[a]

[b]

[c]

[d]

[e]

[f]

# HAM AND CHEESE SCONES

| PREP TIME:<br>20 MINUTES | COOK TIME:<br>20 MINUTES | TOTAL TIME:<br>40 MINUTES | YIELD:<br>8 SCONES |
| --- | --- | --- | --- |

2 cups all-purpose flour

1 tablespoon sugar

1 tablespoon baking powder

1/2 teaspoon garlic powder

1/2 teaspoon kosher salt

1/2 cup (1 stick) cold unsalted butter, cut into cubes

3/4 cup reduced-fat buttermilk

1 cup shredded cheddar cheese

1/3 cup diced ham

2 tablespoons chopped fresh chives

When I grab my morning coffee, I always need a sidekick. Always, always, always. You can never leave your coffee alone. Typically, it's a donut. If it's not a donut, it's a scone.

I don't discriminate when it comes to type. I equally love a blueberry or a pumpkin scone, or a savory ham and cheese scone like this one here.

But the real problem is having only one scone, which is definitely not possible. The combination of ham and cheese is just heaven, especially when you slice them open, warm from the oven, and top them off with two sunny-side-up eggs.

1. Preheat the oven to 425 degrees F. Line a baking sheet with parchment paper or a silicone baking mat.

2. In a large bowl, combine the flour, sugar, baking powder, garlic powder, and salt. Add the cold butter (see photo a), and use your fingers to work the butter into the dry ingredients until it resembles coarse crumbs. Do not overmix.

3. Add the buttermilk, cheese, ham, and chives (photo b) and stir until a soft dough forms.

4. Working on a lightly floured surface, knead the dough 3 or 4 times, until it comes together (photo c). Using a rolling pin, roll the dough into an 8-inch circle, about 1 inch thick (photo d). Cut into 8 wedges using a knife (photo e).

5. Place the scones 1/2 to 1 inch apart on the prepared baking sheet. Bake for 18 to 20 minutes, until firm to the touch and lightly browned (photo f). Serve immediately.

6. TO FREEZE: Place the baked scones on a baking sheet in a single layer and cover tightly with plastic wrap. Freeze overnight. Transfer the scones to freezer bags and freeze for up to 1 month. To serve, defrost at room temperature for 1 hour, then bake at 325 degrees F until warmed, 10 to 15 minutes.

**NUTRITION FACTS:** CALORIES: 303.0 / TOTAL FAT: 17.0 / TRANS FAT: 0.0 / SATURATED FAT: 10.0 / CHOLESTEROL: 52.0 / SODIUM: 513.0 / CARBOHYDRATES: 26.0 / FIBER: 2.0 / SUGAR: 2.0 / PROTEIN: 10.0

# HOMEMADE CRESCENT ROLLS

| PREP TIME: | COOK TIME: | TOTAL TIME: | YIELD: |
|---|---|---|---|
| **3 HOURS** | **15 MINUTES** | **3 ¼ HOURS** | **MAKES 24 ROLLS** |

1¼ cups warm whole milk (105 to 110 degrees F)

½ cup (1 stick) unsalted butter, melted

2 tablespoons honey

2¼ teaspoons active dry yeast

4 cups all-purpose flour, divided

1 large egg

2 teaspoons kosher salt

I admit it. I used those refrigerated crescent tube rolls for years. They just made it too easy, those evil geniuses!

I started to get a lot of requests for a homemade version. After a bunch of recipe testing, recipe fails, and eating about 1,000 crescent rolls, I think we finally nailed it.

The rolls don't require too many ingredients—all you need is time and patience. Everything else is easy-peasy. Promise.

The best part? You can make the dough ahead of time (see the Note). Or, you can freeze the unbaked rolls and bake as needed: Just take out the number of rolls you need from the freezer, let them double in size, and bake. That's it. I told you it was easy!

1. In the bowl of an electric mixer, combine the warm milk, butter, honey, and yeast; let stand until foamy, about 5 minutes.

2. Add 2 cups of the flour, the egg, and salt. Using the dough hook, beat on low speed for 1 to 2 minutes. Add the remaining flour, ½ cup at a time, and beat until a soft, smooth ball of dough forms. The dough should feel elastic and slightly tacky to the touch. Increase the speed to medium-high and beat for 3 minutes.*

3. Lightly oil a large bowl or coat with nonstick spray; place the dough in the bowl, turning to coat. Cover with a clean dishtowel and let stand in a warm spot until the dough has doubled in size, 45 minutes to 1 hour.

*(continued)*

**NOTE**
\* To make the dough ahead of time: Prepare the dough as directed through step 2 and seal in a lightly oiled ziplock bag. Refrigerate for up to 2 days. Resume with step 3.

**NUTRITION FACTS:** CALORIES: 135.0 / TOTAL FAT: 4.0 / TRANS FAT: 0.0 / SATURATED FAT: 3.0 / CHOLESTEROL: 45.0 / SODIUM: 7.0 / CARBOHYDRATES: 20.0 / FIBER: 1.0 / SUGAR: 3.0 / PROTEIN: 2.0

4. Gently deflate the dough by punching it down. Working on a lightly floured surface, divide the dough in half and form each half into a ball. Roll each into a 12-inch round. Cut into 12 wedges. Roll up each wedge, starting from the wide end, to form a crescent shape.

5. Lightly oil a baking sheet or coat with nonstick spray. Place the rolls, point sides down, onto the prepared baking sheet. Cover with a clean dishtowel and let stand in a warm spot until the dough has doubled in size, 30 to 45 minutes.

6. Preheat the oven to 400 degrees F. Brush the roll tops with butter. Bake until golden brown, 12 to 14 minutes. Serve warm.

7. TO FREEZE: Prepare the dough as directed through step 4. Place the rolls in a single layer on a baking sheet and cover tightly with plastic wrap. Freeze overnight. Transfer the rolls to freezer bags and freeze for up to 3 months. Resume with step 5 with the desired number of rolls: Place on prepared baking sheet, loosely cover with plastic wrap, and let the rolls come to room temperature and double in size. Remove the wrap and bake as directed.

# VEGETABLE POTSTICKERS

| PREP TIME: 25 MINUTES | COOK TIME: 15 MINUTES | TOTAL TIME: 40 MINUTES | YIELD: 8 SERVINGS (32 POTSTICKERS) |
|---|---|---|---|

3 tablespoons vegetable oil, divided

1 cup diced shiitake mushrooms

2 shallots, minced

3 cups shredded green cabbage

2 carrots, peeled and grated

½ cup diced water chestnuts

½ cup chopped fresh cilantro leaves

1 large egg, lightly beaten

3 cloves garlic, minced

1 tablespoon freshly grated ginger

1½ tablespoons reduced-sodium soy sauce

1 tablespoon rice wine vinegar

2 teaspoons sesame oil

Kosher salt and freshly ground black pepper, to taste

32 (3-inch) round wonton wrappers

The thing about take-out food is that yes, it's super convenient with all the apps and all, but it can also be very expensive. These potstickers, however, will make you think twice about ordering delivery. They're not only super easy to make, but also fun to make with your kids, getting the whole family involved (even future hubs, Ben). Plus, they are freezer-friendly!

More importantly, this is a completely veggie-loaded meatless filling. Except, really, you won't even miss the meat. With the combination of all the fun veggies and the crunch of the water chestnuts, I prefer this much more than the typical shrimp- or pork-filled ones!

1. Heat 1 tablespoon vegetable oil in a medium skillet over medium-high heat. Add the mushrooms and shallots, and cook, stirring occasionally, until tender, about 3 to 4 minutes. Stir in the cabbage and carrots until tender, about 3 to 5 minutes. Let cool completely.

2. In a large bowl, combine the mushroom mixture, water chestnuts, cilantro, egg, garlic, ginger, soy sauce, rice wine vinegar and sesame oil; season with salt and pepper to taste.

3. To assemble each potsticker, place a wrapper on a work surface. Spoon 1 tablespoon of the mushroom mixture into the center. Using your finger, rub the edges of the wrapper with water. Fold the dough over the filling to create a half-moon shape, pinching the edges to seal.

4. Heat the remaining 2 tablespoons vegetable oil in a large skillet over medium heat. Working in batches, add potstickers in a single layer and cook until the bottoms begin to brown, about 1 minute. Add ¼ cup water, cover, and cook for 2 to 3 minutes; uncover and cook until the liquid has evaporated completely and the bottoms are crisp and golden brown, 3 to 5 more minutes. Repeat with remaining potstickers, adding more vegetable oil as needed. Serve immediately.

*(continued)*

**NUTRITION FACTS:** CALORIES: 213.0 / TOTAL FAT: 5.0 / TRANS FAT: 0.0 / SATURATED FAT: 2.0 / CHOLESTEROL: 27.0 / SODIUM: 449.0 / CARBOHYDRATES: 32.0 / FIBER: 3.0 / SUGAR: 2.0 / PROTEIN: 3.0

5. TO FREEZE: Place uncooked potstickers in a single layer on a baking sheet lined with parchment paper, making sure they are not touching or overlapping. Cover tightly with plastic wrap, and freeze overnight. Transfer the potstickers to freezer bags and freeze for up to 3 months. When ready to cook, there is no need to thaw, but do add 2 minutes to the cooking time. If there is any freezer burn on the potstickers, please be careful when cooking, as the oil may splatter.

# MOM'S POT PIE

| PREP TIME:<br>30 MINUTES | COOK TIME:<br>45 MINUTES | TOTAL TIME:<br>1¼ HOURS | YIELD:<br>6 SERVINGS |
|---|---|---|---|

1 (15-ounce) package refrigerated pie crusts, softened as directed on package

2 tablespoons unsalted butter

2 cloves garlic, minced

⅔ cup diced sweet onion

1 stalk celery, diced

¼ cup all-purpose flour

1¼ teaspoons poultry seasoning

1¾ cups chicken stock

½ cup heavy cream

½ teaspoon dried thyme

3 cups leftover diced rotisserie chicken

1 carrot, peeled and cut into matchsticks

½ cup frozen green peas

2 tablespoons chopped fresh parsley leaves

Kosher salt and freshly ground black pepper, to taste

1 large egg, beaten

Using store-bought pie crust saves you the stress of trying to make the perfect pie crust, and more importantly, saves a ton of time. But the real hero here is that the assembled pie is freezer-friendly! I recommend making two pot pies at a time, one for now and one for that pot-pie fix you'll have in 3 weeks' time.

1. Preheat the oven to 375 degrees F. Line a 9-inch pie plate with one pie crust (reserve the other pie crust for step 4). Trim even with the rim.

2. Melt the butter in a large skillet over medium heat. Add the garlic, onion, and celery and cook, stirring occasionally, until the onion is translucent, about 2 minutes. Whisk in the flour and poultry seasoning and cook until lightly browned, about 1 minute.

3. Gradually whisk in the stock, cream, and thyme. Bring to a boil, stirring constantly. Reduce the heat and simmer until slightly thickened, 2 to 3 minutes. Stir in the chicken, carrot, peas, and parsley; season with salt and pepper.

4. Spoon the mixture into the prepared pie crust and top with the remaining pie crust. Trim, seal, and flute the edges; gently cut 4 or more vents in the top of the crust. Brush the top with the egg.

5. Bake until the crust is golden brown, 40 to 45 minutes. Let cool 10 minutes before serving

6. TO FREEZE: Cover the unbaked pie tightly with plastic wrap and freeze for up to 3 months. To serve, remove from the freezer 30 minutes before baking. Cover loosely with foil and bake at 425 degrees F for 30 minutes. Reduce the temperature to 350 degrees F and bake until the filling is cooked through, reaching an internal temperature of 165 degrees F, 60 to 80 minutes.

**NUTRITION FACTS:** CALORIES: 398.0 / TOTAL FAT: 21.0 / TRANS FAT: 0.0 / SATURATED FAT: 10.0 / CHOLESTEROL: 151.0 / SODIUM: 940.0 / CARBOHYDRATES: 24.0 / FIBER: 0.0 / SUGAR: 3.0 / PROTEIN: 23.0

# ROASTED CAULIFLOWER SOUP

| PREP TIME: 15 MINUTES | COOK TIME: 55 MINUTES | TOTAL TIME: 1 HOUR 10 MINUTES | YIELD: 6 SERVINGS |
|---|---|---|---|

1 head garlic

4 tablespoons olive oil, divided

Kosher salt and freshly ground black pepper, to taste

2 heads cauliflower, cut into florets

1 onion, diced

5 cups vegetable stock, plus more if needed

3 fresh thyme sprigs

1 bay leaf

⅓ cup heavy cream

For the longest time, cauliflower was just one of those vegetables your parents tried to make you eat. It just sat on a plate, steamed with some broccoli or carrots or Brussels sprouts, and you would try to hide it in your dinner napkin. (Or wait, was that just me?)

But I feel like this is the year of the cauliflower. It is really making a name for itself because of all the versatile things you can do with it. It's incredibly healthy for you, so no wonder it is being used everywhere! Even Butters is on the cauliflower train. He always bats my leg with his paw when I am chopping cauliflower, desperate for me to drop a few nuggets down for him.* I rarely ever say no. We all know he's spoiled rotten by me and Ben. But really, we all know it's mostly Ben.

Anyway, more importantly, cauliflower's peak season is fall, which means you can make this soup an amazing part of your holiday cooking. It is also a great cozy meal for cold months when you need extra vitamins and minerals to get you through winter illnesses without adding on those comfort food calories. Or even during the summer when you are looking for a light meal. This is truly an all-season soup!

1. Preheat the oven to 425 degrees F. Lightly oil a baking sheet or coat with nonstick spray.

2. Cut about ¼ inch off the top of the garlic head to expose the tops of the cloves. Place the head, cut side up, on a sheet of foil. Drizzle with 1 tablespoon of the olive oil and season with salt and pepper. Fold up all 4 sides of the foil and wrap tightly.

*(continued)*

**NOTE**
\* Yes, you can certainly feed your dog small amounts of cooked, unseasoned cauliflower (if he or she is not allergic to it). Raw cauliflower is okay but it's more likely to give them gas. So I recommend going the cooked route. Just my two cents!

**NUTRITION FACTS:** CALORIES: 204.0 / TOTAL FAT: 15.0 / TRANS FAT: 0.0 / SATURATED FAT: 4.0 / CHOLESTEROL: 19.0 / SODIUM: 785.0 / CARBOHYDRATES: 15.0 / FIBER: 4.0 / SUGAR: 5.0 / PROTEIN: 6.0

3. Place the cauliflower florets on the prepared baking sheet. Add 2 tablespoons of the olive oil and season with salt and pepper. Gently toss to combine and arrange in a single layer. Place the wrapped garlic head on the baking sheet as well.

4. Roast until the cauliflower is tender and golden brown and the garlic is soft, 30 to 35 minutes. Let cool, then unwrap the garlic and squeeze the garlic from the skins.

5. Heat the remaining 1 tablespoon olive oil in a large stockpot or Dutch oven over medium heat. Add the onion and cook, stirring occasionally, until tender, 3 to 4 minutes. Stir in the stock, thyme, and bay leaf. Bring to a boil, reduce the heat, and simmer, covered, for 5 minutes.

6. Stir in the cauliflower and garlic. Bring to a boil, reduce the heat, and simmer, covered, until the cauliflower is tender and falling apart, about 10 minutes. Remove the bay leaf. Puree the soup with an immersion blender until desired consistency is reached.

7. Stir in the cream and season with salt and pepper to taste. If the soup is too thick, add more stock as needed until desired consistency is reached. Serve immediately.

8. TO FREEZE: Omit the heavy cream until ready to serve. Portion the cooled soup into ziplock freezer bags and lay the bags flat in a single layer in the freezer. Reheat over low heat, stirring occasionally, until heated through.

# ROASTED PUMPKIN SOUP

| PREP TIME: | COOK TIME: | TOTAL TIME: | YIELD: |
|---|---|---|---|
| 15 MINUTES | 1 HOUR | 1¼ HOURS | 6 SERVINGS |

1 (3-pound) sugar pumpkin, halved, seeded, and quartered

2 red bell peppers, quartered

1 Granny Smith apple, quartered and cored

6 fresh thyme sprigs

4 tablespoons olive oil, divided

Kosher salt and freshly ground black pepper, to taste

3 cloves garlic, minced

1 large sweet onion, chopped

4 cups vegetable stock, plus more if needed

6 fresh sage leaves, plus more for garnish

½ cup heavy cream

3 tablespoons pepitas (optional)

I am so BASIC. Like really, really, really BASIC. Because I love pumpkin-anything. The PSLs, the pumpkin donuts, the pumpkin pasta. *All of it.* So it's no surprise that I made a soup out of pumpkin. Because this is *the* perfect soup for those brisk autumn days, topped with pepitas and a beautiful heavy cream swirl. I can just sit by the fireplace in a chunky sweater and sip on this all afternoon with Butters at my feet, keeping them nice and warm.

Except. Well, remember, I already mentioned there really is no need for a working fireplace in Los Angeles. And you get to wear a chunky sweater usually just once each winter. Butters at your feet is also disastrous—because he's a furnace and your feet just sweat and get super clammy.

But the fireplace-pumpkin-soup-plus-corgi image is still nice to think about when you make this soup.

1. Preheat the oven to 400 degrees F. Lightly oil a baking sheet or coat with nonstick spray.

2. Place the pumpkin, bell peppers, apple, and thyme on the prepared baking sheet. Add 2 tablespoons of the olive oil and season with salt and pepper. Gently toss to combine and arrange in a single layer.

3. Roast for 45 to 50 minutes,* stirring halfway through, until the pumpkin is fork-tender. Let cool, then remove the peel from the pumpkin.

4. Heat the remaining 2 tablespoons olive oil in a large stockpot or Dutch oven over medium heat. Add the garlic and onion and cook, stirring occasionally, until tender, 3 to 4 minutes. Stir in the pumpkin, bell peppers, and apple, along with the stock and sage.

*(continued)*

NOTE
* The roasting time may need to be adjusted depending on the size of the pumpkin.

**NUTRITION FACTS:** CALORIES: 268.0 / TOTAL FAT: 18.0 / TRANS FAT: 0.0 / SATURATED FAT: 6.0 / CHOLESTEROL: 31.0 / SODIUM: 539.0 / CARBOHYDRATES: 22.0 / FIBER: 3.0 / SUGAR: 8.0 / PROTEIN: 3.0

5. Bring to a boil; reduce the heat and simmer until the vegetables are tender, 5 to 10 minutes. Puree with an immersion blender.

6. Season with salt and pepper to taste. If the soup is too thick, add more stock as needed until the desired consistency is reached. Portion into serving bowls and swirl in the cream. Serve immediately, garnished with pepitas, sage leaves, and black pepper, if desired.

7. TO FREEZE: Omit the cream and the garnish until ready to serve. Portion the cooled soup into ziplock freezer bags and lay the bags flat in a single layer in the freezer. Reheat over low heat, stirring occasionally, until heated through.

# SLOW COOKER TOMATO BASIL SOUP

| PREP TIME:<br>15 MINUTES | COOK TIME:<br>8 HOURS | TOTAL TIME:<br>8 ¼ HOURS | YIELD:<br>8 SERVINGS |
| --- | --- | --- | --- |

**PARMESAN-CHEDDAR CROUTONS**

4 cups (1-inch) cubes French bread

1 cup shredded extra-sharp cheddar cheese

¼ cup freshly grated Parmesan

2 (28-ounce) cans whole peeled plum tomatoes with basil

1 (15-ounce) can tomato sauce

1½ cups vegetable broth

3 cloves garlic, minced

1 onion, diced

1 red bell pepper, diced

2 tablespoons tomato paste

1½ teaspoons dried oregano

1 teaspoon sugar

½ teaspoon kosher salt

½ teaspoon freshly ground pepper

⅓ cup heavy cream

⅓ cup chopped fresh basil, plus more for garnish

Tomato soup is like the apple pie of soup. It's beloved, it's classic, and it's just simply the best.

I remember my mom used to serve up tomato soup from time to time, particularly on snow days when school was closed. It was the soup from the red cans—and guys, I kid you not: It was perfection. Maybe it was because we were home from school. Or maybe it was because it was −10 degrees F. I don't know. But I have never discriminated against the canned version.

That is, until now, with this slow cooker version. It is just as good, if not better—and has just 219 calories per serving. And that includes the cheesy croutons! Which, by the way, are the best part of the soup anyway.

No, but really, you can simply add all of your ingredients to the slow cooker and let it do its thing for 7 to 8 hours. All you have to do is come home from work and puree with an immersion blender (or in batches with a regular blender, if that's all you have). And it feeds an army, so you'll have tomato soup for weeks!

1. FOR THE CROUTONS: Preheat the oven to 375 degrees F. Lightly oil a baking sheet or coat with nonstick spray.

2. Place the bread cubes on the prepared baking sheet and sprinkle with the cheeses. Arrange in in a single layer and bake until crisp and golden, 10 to 12 minutes, stirring halfway through. Set aside and let cool.

3. Place the tomatoes in a 6-quart slow cooker. Stir in the tomato sauce, broth, garlic, onion, bell pepper, tomato paste, oregano, sugar, salt, and pepper until well combined. Crush the tomatoes into chunks using the back of a spoon.

4. Cover and cook on low heat for 7 to 8 hours or high heat for 3 to 4 hours.

*(continued)*

NUTRITION FACTS: CALORIES: 219.0 / TOTAL FAT: 11.0 / TRANS FAT: 0.0 / SATURATED FAT: 5.0 / CHOLESTEROL: 28.0 / SODIUM: 1023.0 / CARBOHYDRATES: 22.0 / FIBER: 4.0 / SUGAR: 11.0 / PROTEIN: 10.0

5. Puree with an immersion blender until desired consistency is reached. Stir in the cream and basil and season with salt and pepper to taste. Serve immediately with the croutons and basil leaves for garnish.

6. TO FREEZE: Omit the cream and basil until ready to serve. Portion the cooled soup into ziplock freezer bags and lay the bags flat in a single layer in the freezer. The croutons can be stored in ziplock bags or in an airtight container at room temperature for up to 3 days. Reheat the soup over low heat, stirring occasionally, until heated through.

# TURKEY AND VEGGIE LASAGNA

| PREP TIME:<br>20 MINUTES | COOK TIME:<br>45 MINUTES | TOTAL TIME:<br>1 HOUR 5 MINUTES | YIELD:<br>12 SERVINGS |
| --- | --- | --- | --- |

9 whole wheat lasagna noodles

1 tablespoon olive oil

2 cloves garlic, minced

1 onion, diced

2 zucchini, diced

1 carrot, peeled and diced

12 ounces ground turkey

Kosher salt and freshly ground black pepper, to taste

1 (28-ounce) can crushed tomatoes

1 (6-ounce) can tomato paste

1 tablespoon Italian seasoning

1 (15-ounce) package whole milk ricotta

1 (10-ounce) package frozen chopped spinach, thawed and drained

¼ cup freshly grated Parmesan

1 large egg, beaten

2½ cups shredded mozzarella

2 tablespoons chopped fresh parsley leaves (optional)

Guys, I found a way to enjoy lasagna without any of the guilt. I'm serious! Each serving has less than 400 calories! But how is that even possible you may ask?

Well, by using whole wheat lasagna noodles, you get the vitamins, minerals, and fiber that white flour pasta just doesn't have. And ground turkey is a nice change from the ground beef in traditional lasagna. Plus, the turkey really absorbs and takes on the flavors of the sauce and other elements of the lasagna so you won't miss the beef.

The real shocker is that I am keeping the ricotta cheese! First, you can't have a lasagna without it—that is just plain wrong. Second, believe it or not, ricotta is a healthy cheese. It has a ton of protein and about half of your daily recommended calcium intake in one cup. It is also high in vitamins A, B, and zinc.

See, pasta night just got a lot healthier!

1. Preheat the oven to 350 degrees F. Lightly oil a 9x13-inch baking dish or coat with nonstick spray.

2. In a large pot of boiling salted water, cook the lasagna noodles according to package instructions. Drain.

3. Heat the olive oil in a large skillet over medium-high heat. Add the garlic, onion, zucchini, and carrot. Cook, stirring occasionally, until tender, 3 to 4 minutes. Stir in the ground turkey and cook until the turkey has browned, 3 to 5 minutes, making sure to crumble the turkey as it cooks. Season with salt and pepper. Drain excess fat.

4. Stir in the tomatoes, tomato paste, and Italian seasoning until well combined; bring to a simmer and cook until thickened, 8 to 10 minutes.

*(continued)*

NUTRITION FACTS: CALORIES: 391.0 / TOTAL FAT: 19.0 / TRANS FAT: 0.0 / SATURATED FAT: 10.0 / CHOLESTEROL: 95.0 / SODIUM: 614.0 / CARBOHYDRATES: 19.0 / FIBER: 2.0 / SUGAR: 3.0 / PROTEIN: 28.0

5. In a medium bowl, combine the ricotta, spinach, Parmesan, and egg.

6. Spread 1 cup of the meat sauce onto the bottom of the prepared baking dish; top with 3 lasagna noodles, half of the ricotta mixture, and 1 cup mozzarella. Repeat with second layers of sauce, noodles, ricotta, and mozzarella. Top with the remaining noodles and meat sauce, and finally the remaining ½ cup mozzarella cheese.

7. Bake for 35 to 45 minutes, until bubbling. Then broil for 2 to 3 minutes, until the top is browned in spots. Let cool for 15 minutes. Serve, garnished with parsley if desired.

8. TO REFRIGERATE: Cover the unbaked lasagna tightly with plastic wrap and refrigerate for up to 24 hours. To bake, remove the plastic wrap, cover with aluminum foil, and bake at 350 degrees F for 40 minutes. Uncover and bake for an additional 10 to 15 minutes, or until completely cooked through.

9. TO FREEZE: Cover the unbaked lasagna tightly with plastic wrap, then aluminum foil. Freeze for up to 3 months. To bake, remove the plastic wrap, cover with aluminum foil, and bake for 90 minutes. Uncover and bake for an additional 10 to 15 minutes, until completely cooked through.

# WHITE CHICKEN CHILI

| PREP TIME: | COOK TIME: | TOTAL TIME: | YIELD: |
|---|---|---|---|
| **15 MINUTES** | **30 MINUTES** | **45 MINUTES** | **4 SERVINGS** |

1½ tablespoons olive oil

1 small onion, diced

2 large Anaheim green chiles, seeded and diced

1 pound boneless, skinless chicken breasts, cut into 1-inch chunks

Kosher salt and freshly ground black pepper, to taste

2 cloves garlic, minced

1¼ teaspoons ground cumin

1 teaspoon dried oregano

4 cups chicken stock

2 (15-ounce) cans great northern beans, rinsed and drained

3 tablespoons chopped fresh cilantro leaves

1 tablespoon freshly squeezed lime juice

Optional garnishes: Greek yogurt, jalapeño slices, avocado

This is pure comfort in a bowl. Whether it's 107 degrees on a hot LA day, or 24 degrees with a foot of snow in Indiana, this chili delivers in every single way. It's warm, it's cozy, and it doesn't leave you feeling too heavy.

I love using great northern beans because they have a mild flavor that doesn't overpower the flavors of the other ingredients. Plus, beans are a great plant-based protein, high in fiber and full of minerals like iron, potassium, magnesium, and phosphorus.

This is basically a bowl of true comfort, plenty of protein, and 316 calories per serving.

1. Heat the olive oil in a large stockpot or Dutch oven over medium heat. Add the onion and chiles and cook, stirring frequently, until the onions are translucent, 2 to 3 minutes.

2. Season the chicken with salt and pepper. Add the chicken to the pot and cook until golden, 3 to 4 minutes. Stir in the garlic, cumin, and oregano and cook until fragrant, about 1 minute. Stir in the stock, scraping any browned bits from the bottom of the pot.

3. Stir in the beans. Bring to a boil; cover, reduce the heat, and simmer for 15 minutes. Uncover and continue to simmer until slightly reduced, 5 to 10 minutes. Using a potato masher, mash the beans until smooth or the desired consistency is reached.

4. Stir in the cilantro and lime juice and season with salt and pepper to taste. Serve immediately, with additional garnishes if desired.

5. TO FREEZE: Omit the garnishes until ready to serve. Portion the cooled chili into ziplock freezer bags and lay the bags flat in a single layer in the freezer. Reheat over low heat, stirring occasionally, until heated through.

**NUTRITION FACTS:** CALORIES: 316.0 / TOTAL FAT: 6.0 / TRANS FAT: 0.0 / SATURATED FAT: 1.0 / CHOLESTEROL: 65.0 / SODIUM: 1353.0 / CARBOHYDRATES: 34.0 / FIBER: 11.0 / SUGAR: 1.0 / PROTEIN: 32.0

MEAL PREP
CHICKEN—3 WAYS

# 10. Dinner

# ASIAN GARLIC-CHICKEN LETTUCE WRAPS

| PREP TIME: 15 MINUTES | COOK TIME: 10 MINUTES | TOTAL TIME: 25 MINUTES | YIELD: 4 SERVINGS |
|---|---|---|---|

2 tablespoons reduced-sodium soy sauce

2 tablespoons freshly squeezed lime juice

1½ tablespoons fish sauce

1½ tablespoons light brown sugar

1½ tablespoons chili garlic sauce

1½ tablespoons canola oil

1 pound ground chicken breast

2 shallots, minced

1 red bell pepper, diced

3 cloves garlic, minced

1 tablespoon freshly grated ginger

¼ cup chopped fresh cilantro leaves

Freshly ground black pepper, to taste

1 head butter lettuce

¼ cup peanuts, chopped (optional)

If you've followed me for a while, you know that I have a huge love affair with donuts. Thanks to that obsession, I need to cut down on the carbs and calories as much as possible during other meal-times to make up for donut intake. Hence, we have lettuce wraps, a perfect way to cut out calories from otherwise heavy dishes, with just 246 calories and 13 grams of carbs per serving.

The key to a perfect lettuce wrap starts with the filling; but more importantly, it's about the perfect lettuce. Pick large, firm, pliable leaves so you don't have to worry about spillage or breakage. Nobody wants to chase around the small fallen bits on their plate with flimsy lettuce!

1. In a small bowl, whisk together the soy sauce, lime juice, fish sauce, brown sugar, and chili garlic sauce; set aside.

2. Heat the canola oil in a large skillet over medium-high heat. Add the ground chicken, shallots, and bell pepper and cook until the chicken is browned and completely cooked through, 3 to 5 minutes, making sure to crumble the chicken as it cooks; drain excess fat. Stir in the garlic and ginger and cook until fragrant, about 1 minute.

3. Stir in the soy sauce mixture and cook until slightly reduced, about 2 minutes. Remove from the heat. Stir in the cilantro and season with pepper.

4. Divide the chicken mixture into meal prep containers. Refrigerate for up to 3 days.

5. To serve, spoon several tablespoons of the chicken mixture into the center of a lettuce leaf, taco-style, and garnish with peanuts if desired.

**NUTRITION FACTS:** CALORIES: 246.0 / TOTAL FAT: 17.0 / TRANS FAT: 0.0 / SATURATED FAT: 3.0 / CHOLESTEROL: 37.0 / SODIUM: 997.0 / CARBOHYDRATES: 13.0 / FIBER: 2.0 / SUGAR: 5.0 / PROTEIN: 15.0

# FARRO BIBIMBAP BOWLS

| PREP TIME: 25 MINUTES | COOK TIME: 30 MINUTES | TOTAL TIME: 55 MINUTES | YIELD: 4 SERVINGS |
|---|---|---|---|

²/₃ cup farro

4 medium eggs*

1 tablespoon olive oil

2 cloves garlic, minced

4 cups chopped spinach

1 cup bean sprouts

2 carrots, peeled and spiralized

1 batch Korean Beef (page 135)

2 zucchini, peeled and spiralized

1 cup kimchi

2 green onions, thinly sliced (optional)

4 teaspoons gochujang (optional)

1 teaspoon toasted sesame seeds (optional)

As corny as it sounds, I truly feel that really good food is always possible when you cook from the heart. When someone makes a dish that is near and dear to their heart, whether it is from a family recipe from 100 years ago or something they made for a partner on a first date, you can taste the love they put into the dish.

One of those recipes for me is bibimbap. This is a Korean dish I grew up on, a staple in our household, where my mom's version would be the absolute best. I've tried to re-create her bibimbap but my attempts have never compared with hers. She's got some secret bibimbap potion, I think.

But even without her potion, I've put the Damn Delicious spin to it, using my favorite, and very popular, Korean beef as the protein base. But it's also loaded with so many veggies that it can truly be a clean-out-the-fridge-type meal. And don't worry. Kimchi is readily available at many grocery stores now.

1. Cook the farro according to package instructions; set aside.

2. Place the eggs in a large saucepan and cover with cold water by 1 inch. Bring to a boil and cook for 1 minute. Cover the pot with a tight-fitting lid and remove from the heat; let sit for 8 to 10 minutes. Drain well and let cool before peeling and halving.

3. Heat the olive oil in a large skillet over medium-high heat. Add the garlic and cook, stirring frequently, until fragrant, 1 to 2 minutes. Stir in the spinach and cook until wilted, 2 to 3 minutes; set aside. In the same pan, stir-fry the bean sprouts until just tender, about 2 minutes; set aside.

4. Divide the farro into meal prep containers. Top with the Korean beef, eggs, spinach, bean sprouts, carrots, zucchini, and kimchi. Garnish with green onions, gochujang, and sesame seeds, if desired. Will keep in the refrigerator 3 to 4 days.

NOTE

* If serving immediately, runny, sunny-side-up eggs are perfect. But for meal prep purposes, the hard-boiled eggs are best.

NUTRITION FACTS: CALORIES: 485.0 / TOTAL FAT: 21.0 / TRANS FAT: 0.0 / SATURATED FAT: 5.0 / CHOLESTEROL: 156.0 / SODIUM: 1088.0 / CARBOHYDRATES: 52.0 / FIBER: 9.0 / SUGAR: 15.0 / PROTEIN: 33.0

# GENERAL TSO'S CAULIFLOWER

| PREP TIME:<br>15 MINUTES | COOK TIME:<br>45 MINUTES | TOTAL TIME:<br>1 HOUR | YIELD:<br>4 SERVINGS |
| --- | --- | --- | --- |

1 cup brown rice

1 large head cauliflower, cut into florets

1 tablespoon canola oil

3 tablespoons cornstarch, divided

2/3 cup vegetable broth

3 tablespoons reduced-sodium soy sauce

3 tablespoons light brown sugar

1½ tablespoons seasoned rice vinegar

2 teaspoons toasted sesame oil

1 shallot, minced

3 cloves garlic, minced

1 tablespoon freshly grated ginger

¼ teaspoon crushed red pepper flakes (optional)

2 green onions, thinly sliced

2 teaspoons toasted sesame seeds

Let's be honest, when ordering Chinese takeout, how many of us actually get something new? If you are anything like me, you end up ordering the same thing every time. And as riveting as it is, I always end up ordering the General Tso's chicken. It's basic, but it's also too good to pass up.

But we all know that this isn't the healthiest choice on the menu, so I am taking everyone's favorite go-to dish and giving it a huge makeover.

We're swapping out the chicken and using cauliflower instead. It's much more affordable, and it's perfect for Meatless Mondays. Cauliflower is also the most versatile vegetable around. It's consistency and ability to take on great flavors make it the perfect meat substitute.

Serve over a bed of brown rice and I promise: As in the Vegetable Potstickers on page 219, you won't be missing the meat in this at all!

1. Cook the rice according to package instructions; set aside.

2. Preheat the oven to 450 degrees F. Lightly oil a baking sheet or coat with nonstick spray.

3. Place the cauliflower florets on the prepared baking sheet. Add the canola oil and 2 tablespoons of the cornstarch and gently toss to combine. Arrange in a single layer and bake for 20 to 25 minutes, until tender and golden brown.

4. In a medium bowl, whisk together the broth, soy sauce, brown sugar, rice vinegar, and the remaining 1 tablespoon cornstarch; set aside.

*(continued)*

**NUTRITION FACTS:** CALORIES: 307.0 / TOTAL FAT: 6.0 / TRANS FAT: 0.0 / SATURATED FAT: 0.0 / CHOLESTEROL: 0.0 / SODIUM: 635.0 / CARBOHYDRATES: 50.0 / FIBER: 6.0 / SUGAR: 5.0 / PROTEIN: 8.0

5. Heat the sesame oil in a large skillet over medium heat. Add the shallot and cook, stirring frequently, until golden, about 2 minutes. Stir in the garlic, ginger, and red pepper flakes (if using) and cook until fragrant, about 1 minute.

6. Stir in the broth mixture; reduce the heat and simmer, whisking constantly, until thickened, 1 to 2 minutes. Stir in the cauliflower, green onions, and sesame seeds.

7. Divide the rice and cauliflower mixture into meal prep containers. Will keep in the refrigerator 3 to 4 days. Reheat in the microwave in 30-second intervals until heated through.

# MEAL PREP CHICKEN—3 WAYS

Remember when I said that meal prep didn't have to mean bland, dry chicken?

Well, I meant every single word. And to prove it, I have your very own meal prep chicken in three different, yet all equally amazing, versions.

In each variation, the chicken comes out perfectly tender, juicy, and packed with a punch in its own way—whether it's Asian flair with a spicy kick to it, a sweet punch from an all-American honey mustard sauce, or a spritely boost from lime and cilantro.

All you need is boneless, skinless chicken breasts (thighs will also work!), plus your choice of three simple marinades. Just let the chicken marinate overnight. Then, when you're ready for dinner, all that's left to do is a simple stir-fry. Add your desired vegetables like kale, spinach, broccoli, and/or bell peppers to dress it up, and serve with your preferred grain. Farro is my favorite right now, but brown rice or quinoa would also work!

## Spicy Korean Sesame Chicken

| PREP TIME: 45 MINUTES | COOK TIME: 10 MINUTES | TOTAL TIME: 55 MINUTES | YIELD: 4 SERVINGS |
|---|---|---|---|

1½ pounds boneless, skinless chicken breasts, cut into 1-inch chunks

½ cup diced onion

4 tablespoons gochujang sauce, divided

3 cloves garlic, minced

1 tablespoon seasoned rice wine vinegar

2 teaspoons sesame oil

Kosher salt and freshly ground black pepper, to taste

1 tablespoon canola oil

3 tablespoons chicken stock

1 teaspoon toasted sesame seeds

1. In a gallon-size ziplock bag, combine the chicken, onion, 3 tablespoons of the gochujang, the garlic, vinegar, and sesame oil; season with salt and pepper. Marinate for at least 30 minutes (or up to overnight in the fridge), turning the bag occasionally. Drain the chicken and discard the marinade.

2. Heat the canola oil in a large skillet over medium-high heat. Working in batches, add the chicken and cook until golden brown, 4 to 5 minutes. Stir in the stock and cook, stirring and scraping up the browned bits with a wooden spoon. Remove from heat. Stir in the remaining 1 tablespoon gochujang and the sesame seeds, and season with salt and pepper to taste.

3. Place into meal prep containers with veggies and grain of choice. Will keep in the refrigerator 3 to 4 days. Reheat in the microwave in 30-second intervals until heated through.

**NUTRITION FACTS:** CALORIES: 176.0 / TOTAL FAT: 9.0 / TRANS FAT: 0.0 / SATURATED FAT: 0.0 / CHOLESTEROL: 54.0 / SODIUM: 699.0 / CARBOHYDRATES: 6.0 / FIBER: 0.0 / SUGAR: 5.0 / PROTEIN: 17.0

SPICY KOREAN
SESAME CHICKEN

CILANTRO LIME
CHICKEN

HONEY MUSTARD
CHICKEN

# Honey Mustard Chicken

| PREP TIME: **45 MINUTES** | COOK TIME: **10 MINUTES** | TOTAL TIME: **55 MINUTES** | YIELD: **4 SERVINGS** |
|---|---|---|---|

1½ pounds boneless, skinless chicken breasts, cut into 1-inch chunks

½ cup diced onion

2 tablespoons whole grain mustard

1 clove garlic, minced

2 tablespoons olive oil, divided

Kosher salt and freshly ground black pepper, to taste

3 tablespoons chicken stock

2 tablespoons honey

1. In a gallon-size ziplock bag, combine the chicken, onion, mustard, garlic, and 1 tablespoon of the olive oil; season with salt and pepper. Marinate for at least 30 minutes (or up to overnight in the fridge), turning the bag occasionally. Drain the chicken and discard the marinade.

2. Heat the remaining 1 tablespoon olive oil in a large skillet over medium-high heat. Working in batches, add the chicken and cook until golden brown, 4 to 5 minutes. Stir in the stock and cook, stirring and scraping up the browned bits with a wooden spoon. Remove from the heat. Stir in the honey until the chicken is evenly coated; season with salt and pepper to taste.

3. Place into meal prep containers with veggies and grain of choice. Will keep in the refrigerator 3 to 4 days. Reheat in the microwave in 30-second intervals until heated through.

**NUTRITION FACTS:** CALORIES: 176.0 / TOTAL FAT: 9.0 / TRANS FAT: 0.0 / SATURATED FAT: 2.0 / CHOLESTEROL: 54.0 / SODIUM: 553.0 / CARBOHYDRATES: 11.0 / FIBER: 0.0 / SUGAR: 10.0 / PROTEIN: 17.0

# Cilantro Lime Chicken

| PREP TIME: **45 MINUTES** | COOK TIME: **10 MINUTES** | TOTAL TIME: **55 MINUTES** | YIELD: **4 SERVINGS** |
|---|---|---|---|

1½ pounds boneless, skinless chicken breasts, cut into 1-inch chunks

½ cup diced onion

2 cloves garlic, minced

¾ teaspoon ground cumin

2 teaspoons grated lime zest

2 tablespoons freshly squeezed lime juice, divided

4 tablespoons chopped fresh cilantro leaves, divided

2 tablespoons olive oil, divided

Kosher salt and freshly ground black pepper, to taste

1. In a gallon-size ziplock bag, combine the chicken, onion, garlic, cumin, lime zest, 1 tablespoon of the lime juice, 2 tablespoons of the cilantro, and 1 tablespoon of the olive oil. Season with salt and pepper. Marinate for at least 30 minutes (or up to overnight in the fridge), turning the bag occasionally. Drain the chicken and discard the marinade.

2. Heat the remaining 1 tablespoon olive oil in a large skillet over medium-high heat. Working in batches, add the chicken and cook until golden brown, 4 to 5 minutes. Remove from the heat. Stir in the remaining 2 tablespoons cilantro and 1 tablespoon lime juice; season with salt and pepper to taste.

3. Place into meal prep containers with veggies and grain of choice. Will keep in the refrigerator 3 to 4 days. Reheat in the microwave in 30-second intervals until heated through.

**NUTRITION FACTS:** CALORIES: 162.0 / TOTAL FAT: 9.0 / TRANS FAT: 0.0 / SATURATED FAT: 2.0 / CHOLESTEROL: 54.0 / SODIUM: 432.0 / CARBOHYDRATES: 3.0 / FIBER: 0.0 / SUGAR: 1.0 / PROTEIN: 17.0

# QUINOA CHILI

| PREP TIME: | COOK TIME: | TOTAL TIME: | YIELD: |
|---|---|---|---|
| 15 MINUTES | 45 MINUTES | 1 HOUR | 8 SERVINGS |

1 cup quinoa

1 tablespoon olive oil

3 cloves garlic, minced

1 onion, diced

2 (14.5-ounce) cans diced tomatoes

1 (15-ounce) can tomato sauce

1 (4.5-ounce) can diced green chiles

1½ tablespoons chili powder, or more to taste

2 teaspoons ground cumin

1½ teaspoons paprika

½ teaspoon cayenne pepper

Kosher salt and freshly ground black pepper, to taste

1 (15-ounce) can kidney beans, drained and rinsed

1 (15-ounce) can black beans, drained and rinsed

1½ cups corn kernels (frozen, canned, or roasted)

3 tablespoons chopped fresh cilantro leaves

Juice of 1 lime (optional)

6 tablespoons Greek yogurt (optional)

6 tablespoons shredded reduced-fat cheddar cheese (optional)

Yes, you can absolutely still get that comforting chili fix without any of the heavy calories. Not to mention the triple-threat protein punch of quinoa, black beans, and kidney beans here! And even though it's only 301 calories per bowl, it still tastes pretty damn great.

Plus, we can still have fun with our garnishes. You can add a dollop of Greek yogurt (instead of sour cream), cheddar cheese, and fresh cilantro if you like. And a little bit of freshly squeezed lime juice on top goes a long way.

1. Cook the quinoa in a large saucepan with 2 cups water according to package instructions; set aside.

2. Heat the olive oil in a Dutch oven or large pot over medium-high heat. Add the garlic and onion and cook, stirring frequently, until the onion is translucent, 2 to 3 minutes. Stir in the quinoa, diced tomatoes, tomato sauce, green chiles, chili powder, cumin, paprika, cayenne pepper, and 1 to 2 cups water, making sure to cover most of the ingredients; season with salt and pepper. Reduce the heat to low; cover and simmer until thickened, about 30 minutes.

3. Stir in the kidney and black beans, and the corn, cilantro, and lime juice (if using), and cook until heated through, about 2 minutes.

4. Serve immediately, garnished with Greek yogurt and cheese, if desired. Or let cool, divide into meal prep jars. Will keep in the refrigerator 3 to 4 days. Reheat in the microwave in 30-second intervals until heated through.

**NUTRITION FACTS:** CALORIES: 301.0 / TOTAL FAT: 7.0 / TRANS FAT: 0.0 / SATURATED FAT: 2.0 / CHOLESTEROL: 3.0 / SODIUM: 752.0 / CARBOHYDRATES: 42.0 / FIBER: 11.0 / SUGAR: 9.0 / PROTEIN: 10.0

# SHEET PAN MISO SALMON DINNER

| PREP TIME:<br>15 MINUTES | COOK TIME:<br>15 MINUTES | TOTAL TIME:<br>30 MINUTES | YIELD:<br>4 SERVINGS |
|---|---|---|---|

2 tablespoons white miso paste

1 tablespoon seasoned rice wine vinegar

2 teaspoons reduced-sodium soy sauce

2 teaspoons honey

1½ teaspoons chili garlic sauce

4 (6-ounce) salmon fillets

3 baby bok choy, separated into leaves

1 red bell pepper, cut into ¾-inch strips

6 green onions, cut into 1½-inch pieces

2 teaspoons canola oil

2 teaspoons toasted sesame oil

Kosher salt and freshly ground black pepper, to taste

This is probably one of the speediest meals in the entire book. It requires just 15 minutes prep and 15 minutes cooking. It also cooks on one sheet pan…so hello, you have the easiest cleanup in the world here. Not to mention, salmon is one of the healthiest foods you can eat. It is chock-full of all those omega-3 fatty acids that are crucial for your heart health.

The miso paste is also such a huge part of this recipe. It's another underused ingredient, but it's one of my favorites. It packs a punch with its strong flavor, so a little will go a long way. And when you combine it with rice vinegar, soy sauce, chili garlic sauce, and a bit of honey to sweeten it, the end result is an incredible, irresistible marinade for salmon.

1. Preheat the oven to 475 degrees F. Lightly oil a baking sheet or coat with nonstick spray.

2. In a small bowl, whisk together the miso, rice wine vinegar, soy sauce, honey, and chili garlic sauce.

3. Place the salmon on one side of the prepared baking sheet. Spoon the miso mixture over the salmon. Bake for 5 minutes.

4. Working quickly, place the bok choy, bell pepper, and green onions on the opposite side of the baking sheet. Add the canola oil and sesame oil and season with salt and pepper. Gently toss to combine and arrange in a single layer.

5. Bake until the fish flakes easily with a fork and vegetables are crisp-tender, 8 to 10 minutes more.

6. Portion the fish and veggies into meal prep containers and store in the refrigerator for up to 3 days. Reheat in the microwave in 30-second intervals until heated through.

**NUTRITION FACTS:** CALORIES: 253.0 / TOTAL FAT: 11.0 / TRANS FAT: 0.0 / SATURATED FAT: 3.0 / CHOLESTEROL: 74.0 / SODIUM: 1106.0 / CARBOHYDRATES: 11.0 / FIBER: 3.0 / SUGAR: 7.0 / PROTEIN: 31.0

# SHRIMP SCAMPI SPAGHETTI SQUASH

| PREP TIME: | COOK TIME: | TOTAL TIME: | YIELD: |
|---|---|---|---|
| 20 MINUTES | 45 MINUTES | 1 HOUR 5 MINUTES | 4 SERVINGS |

**SPAGHETTI SQUASH**

1 (2- to 3-pound) spaghetti squash

2 tablespoons olive oil

Kosher salt and freshly ground black pepper, to taste

1¼ pounds large shrimp, peeled and deveined

1½ teaspoons smoked paprika

Kosher salt and freshly ground black pepper, to taste

2 tablespoons unsalted butter

3 cloves garlic, minced

1 shallot, minced

3 cups baby spinach

½ cup fresh basil leaves, chiffonade

1 tablespoon freshly squeezed lemon juice

3 tablespoons freshly grated Parmesan (optional)

Pasta is my ultimate weakness. It's incredibly versatile and it just goes well with anything and everything, particularly Parmesan. Except, the calories/carbs just keep adding up!

But fret no more. Spaghetti squash is here for the calorie-carb rescue! By using spaghetti squash, you cut down the calories by about 75 percent. And it also provides other health boosts like vitamin A and potassium! Just be sure to pick the right squash: It should be pale yellow in color and hard with no tender spots.

The shrimp, garlic, and shallots flavor the squash just beautifully here. I love to add a bit of fresh basil, lemon juice, and some Parmesan. With all these goodies, you won't miss the pasta at all. Plus, each serving has only 201 calories!

1. FOR THE SQUASH: Preheat the oven to 375 degrees F. Lightly oil a baking sheet or coat with nonstick spray.

2. Cut the squash in half lengthwise from stem to tail and scrape out the seeds. Drizzle with the olive oil and season with salt and pepper. Place cut side down on the prepared baking dish and roast until tender, 35 to 45 minutes. Let rest until cool enough to handle.

3. Using a fork, scrape the flesh to create long strands and set aside.

4. Season the shrimp with the paprika, salt, and pepper. Melt the butter in a large skillet over medium-high heat. Add the shrimp, garlic, and shallot and cook, stirring occasionally, until the shrimp is pink, 2 to 3 minutes. Transfer to a bowl and keep warm.

5. In the same skillet, cook the squash and spinach, stirring occasionally, until the squash is heated through and the spinach has wilted, 2 to 3 minutes. Stir in the basil and lemon juice, and season with salt and pepper to taste.

6. Serve immediately, topping the squash with the shrimp and garnishing with Parmesan, if desired. Or portion into meal prep containers and store in the refrigerator for up to 3 days. Reheat in the microwave in 30-second intervals until heated through.

**NUTRITION FACTS:** CALORIES: 201.0 / TOTAL FAT: 20.0 / TRANS FAT: 0.0 / SATURATED FAT: 7.0 / CHOLESTEROL: 228.0 / SODIUM: 1544.0 / CARBOHYDRATES: 10.0 / FIBER: 2.0 / SUGAR: 3.0 / PROTEIN: 26.0

# THAI BASIL CHICKEN BOWLS

| PREP TIME: 15 MINUTES | COOK TIME: 30 MINUTES | TOTAL TIME: 45 MINUTES | YIELD: 4 SERVINGS |
| --- | --- | --- | --- |

1 cup jasmine rice

½ cup chicken stock

3 tablespoons reduced-sodium soy sauce

1 tablespoon fish sauce

1½ tablespoons light brown sugar

1½ tablespoons unseasoned rice vinegar

2 tablespoons vegetable oil

3 cloves garlic, minced

2 shallots, thinly sliced

1 red Thai chile pepper, thinly sliced

1¼ pounds ground chicken breast

1½ cups packed fresh basil leaves

If I had to choose one recipe from this entire book to cook tonight, it would be this one. Hands down. It's one of those short-ingredient-list, quick-stir-fry dinners that just knock it out of the park. Because at the end of the day, simple is best, and that's exactly what we have here.

We start with crumbling some ground chicken breast (turkey is also a great substitute), then stirring in a super-simple sauce base that packs such a punch. And the red Thai chile pepper adds just enough heat without being too overpowering. But you can be as heavy- or light-handed as you like. It just depends on your tolerance.

Serve with jasmine rice to have the easiest, simplest, and heartiest dinner at fewer than 400 calories per serving. That's 397, to be exact.

1. Cook the rice according to package instructions; set aside.

2. In a small bowl, whisk together the stock, soy sauce, fish sauce, brown sugar, and vinegar; set aside.

3. Heat the vegetable oil in a large skillet over medium heat. Add the garlic, shallots, and chile. Cook, stirring frequently, until fragrant, 1 to 2 minutes. Add the ground chicken and cook until browned and cooked through, 3 to 5 minutes, making sure to crumble the chicken as it cooks; drain excess fat.

4. Stir in the stock mixture and cook over medium heat, stirring constantly, until the sauce has thickened, 2 to 3 minutes. Stir in the basil until just wilted, about 30 seconds.

5. Divide the rice into bowls and top with the chicken mixture. Or portion into meal prep bowls and refrigerate for 3 to 4 days. Reheat in the microwave in 30-second intervals until heated through.

**NUTRITION FACTS:** CALORIES: 397.0 / TOTAL FAT: 10.0 / TRANS FAT: 0.0 / SATURATED FAT: 2.0 / CHOLESTEROL: 55.0 / SODIUM: 1152.0 / CARBOHYDRATES: 38.0 / FIBER: 0.0 / SUGAR: 3.0 / PROTEIN: 21.0

# SKINNY GUMBO

| PREP TIME: | COOK TIME: | TOTAL TIME: | YIELD: |
|---|---|---|---|
| **15 MINUTES** | **30 MINUTES** | **45 MINUTES** | **4 SERVINGS** |

1 cup basmati rice

¼ cup all-purpose flour

1 tablespoon olive oil

3 cloves garlic, minced

1 sweet onion, diced

1 green bell pepper, chopped

1 stalk celery, diced

6 ounces smoked andouille sausage, thinly sliced

1½ teaspoons Cajun seasoning

¼ cup dry white wine*

2 cups chicken stock

1 (14.5-ounce) can diced tomatoes

1 pound medium shrimp, peeled and deveined

1 cup cut fresh or frozen okra (optional)

2 tablespoons chopped fresh parsley leaves

Kosher salt and freshly ground black pepper, to taste

2 green onions, thinly sliced (optional)

I was fortunate enough to visit New Orleans recently. I admit, I only went to Louisiana for two reasons: beignets and gumbo. But to be honest, I never actually had gumbo until I arrived in New Orleans! I have been living in Los Angeles for 18 years—our diets consisted of all the new health trends, so basically kale, acai bowls, and protein shakes as of now.

So, to make up for the first 30 years of my life being gumbo-less, I've actually been making it right at home. A meal prep–friendly version that's light enough to eat often (and is perfect for balancing out those donut-filled days).

Now the key to a successful gumbo is the thickness of the stew, so that's why we add the flour. I like to toast it a bit before using it to thicken the stock as it adds that nutty, more complex flavor. Just know that the longer the flour is cooked, the deeper the flavor. I know it seems like a trivial step but it will make all the difference in the world.

1. Cook the rice according to package instructions in a large saucepan of 2 cups water; set aside.

2. Cook the flour in a dry large stockpot or Dutch oven over medium-high heat, whisking constantly, until golden brown, 6 to 10 minutes; set aside.

3. Heat the olive oil in the stockpot. Add the garlic, onion, bell pepper, celery, and sausage and cook, stirring frequently, until the sausage is lightly browned, 5 to 7 minutes. Stir in the Cajun seasoning and cook until fragrant, about 1 minute.

*(continued)*

**NOTE**
\* Additional chicken stock can be used as a non-alcoholic substitute for the wine.

**NUTRITION FACTS:** CALORIES: 492.0 / TOTAL FAT: 17.0 / TRANS FAT: 0.0 / SATURATED FAT: 5.0 / CHOLESTEROL: 141.0 / SODIUM: 1867.0 / CARBOHYDRATES: 53.0 / FIBER: 4.0 / SUGAR: 6.0 / PROTEIN: 38.0

4. Stir in the wine, scraping any browned bits from the bottom of the stockpot. Stir in the flour, stock, and diced tomatoes until well combined. Bring to a boil; reduce the heat and simmer for 10 minutes.

5. Stir in the shrimp and okra, if using. Continue to simmer until the shrimp is cooked through and the okra is tender, 3 to 4 minutes. Stir in the parsley and season with salt and pepper to taste.

6. Portion into meal prep bowls with the rice; garnish with green onions, if desired. Will keep in the refrigerator 3 to 4 days. Reheat in the microwave in 30-second intervals until heated through.

# HAMBURGER STEAK TV DINNER

| PREP TIME: | COOK TIME: | TOTAL TIME: | YIELD: |
|---|---|---|---|
| **20 MINUTES** | **20 MINUTES** | **40 MINUTES** | **4 SERVINGS** |

1¼ pounds ground sirloin

1 teaspoon Worcestershire sauce

Kosher salt and freshly ground black pepper, to taste

2 teaspoons olive oil

2 cloves garlic, minced

1 large sweet onion, thinly sliced

1 tablespoon all-purpose flour

1 cup beef stock

¼ cup dry white wine

1 tablespoon chopped fresh thyme

¾ pound green beans, trimmed

2 teaspoons unsalted butter, melted

¾ teaspoon garlic salt

2 cups Slow Cooker Cauliflower Mashed Potatoes (page 268)

I love the idea of a TV dinner. It's typically something really comforting, like meatloaf or fried chicken. Plus, you have multiple compartments, which means, hello, multiple side dishes. Except, we all know that pre-packed frozen meals don't provide the best nutritional balance.

The basic ingredients of a classic TV dinner are meat, potatoes, and a vegetable. We've got those covered. See below.

For the meat, we have the most tender, melt-in-your-mouth-type of hamburger steak. Now the key to this is the kind of meat you use. In this case, it's ground sirloin. It is a little bit pricier but it will be well worth it. Trust me.

For potatoes, we're using my favorite cauliflower mashed potatoes. They are a step up in flavor and nutrients from your traditional mashed potatoes. And cauliflower is full of vitamins B, C, and K. Not to mention, this mash has about one-fourth the calories of traditional mashed potatoes!

For the veggies, well, we already have cauliflower from the potatoes (two birds, one stone), and then we have green beans!

But really, can we talk about that gravy now? The garlic and onions pack the gravy with a ton of flavor, as does using fresh thyme. But I always need extra onions in my gravy. Always, always, always.

So get ready to pop in your favorite movie or TV show (*Grey's Anatomy* on repeat, of course!) and curl up on the couch with an actual TV dinner that has only 334 calories per serving!

1. In a large bowl, combine the ground sirloin with the Worcestershire sauce; season with ¼ teaspoon salt and ¼ teaspoon pepper, or more to taste. Divide into 4 portions and shape into patties.

*(continued)*

**NUTRITION FACTS:** CALORIES: 334.0 / TOTAL FAT: 15.0 / TRANS FAT: 0.0 / SATURATED FAT: 4.0 / CHOLESTEROL: 80.0 / SODIUM: 765.0 / CARBOHYDRATES: 16.0 / FIBER: 2.0 / SUGAR: 3.0 / PROTEIN: 25.0

2. Heat the olive oil in a large skillet over medium-high heat. Add the patties and cook, turning once, until browned, about 3 minutes per side. Transfer the patties to a plate and set aside.

3. Add the garlic and onion to the skillet and cook, stirring frequently, until translucent, 2 to 3 minutes. Whisk in the flour until lightly browned, about 30 seconds.

4. Stir in the stock, wine, and thyme. Bring to a boil and return the patties to the skillet. Reduce the heat and simmer, partially covered, until the sauce is slightly thickened and the patties are completely cooked through, reaching an internal temperature of 160 degrees F, 7 to 10 minutes.

5. In a large pot of boiling salted water, blanch the green beans until bright green in color, about 2 minutes. Drain well and cool in a bowl of ice water. Drain well. Stir the melted butter and garlic salt into the beans and season with salt and pepper to taste.

6. Place the patties, green beans, and cauliflower mashed potatoes into meal prep containers. Will keep in the refrigerator 3 to 4 days. Reheat in the microwave in 30-second intervals until cooked through.

# FRIED CHICKEN TV DINNER

| PREP TIME: | COOK TIME: | TOTAL TIME: | YIELD: |
|:---:|:---:|:---:|:---:|
| 30 MINUTES | 30 MINUTES | 1 HOUR | 4 SERVINGS |

4 boneless, skinless chicken thighs, excess fat trimmed

Kosher salt and freshly ground black pepper, to taste

2½ cups cornflake cereal, crushed

3 tablespoons freshly grated Parmesan

1 tablespoon vegetable oil

½ teaspoon paprika

½ cup buttermilk

⅓ cup all-purpose flour

1½ cups corn kernels (frozen, canned, or roasted)

2 cups Slow Cooker Cauliflower Mashed Potatoes (page 268)

Everyone loves fried chicken, right? I mean, have you had KFC? That was a Friday night staple for us in my family when I was growing up. We had the family-size fried chicken bucket with coleslaw and *extra* biscuits. It was a weekend treat, and a break from all the kimchi stews my mom made.

But we all know that chicken cooked in a vat of oil really isn't going to do the body any good. And when you make it at home, it leaves a mess. So, I always opt for baked "fried" chicken. It's cleaner for your body, and your kitchen.

By using vegetable oil, Parmesan, paprika, and cornflakes, you get a really nice crunch on the outside of the chicken without actually deep-frying. It's genius. I know.

Cauliflower mashed potatoes make the perfect side. They're so much healthier than just potatoes, and cauliflower helps in digestion and decreases the risk for heart disease.

So there you have it. A hearty fried chicken TV dinner that is actually good for the heart!

1. Preheat the oven to 425 degrees F. Line a baking sheet with parchment paper or a silicone baking mat.

2. Season the chicken thighs with salt and pepper.

3. In a large shallow bowl, combine the cornflakes, Parmesan, vegetable oil, and paprika. Place the buttermilk in a second bowl and the flour in a third.

4. Working one at a time—using an assembly line method—dredge the chicken in the flour, dip into the buttermilk, then dredge in the cornflake mixture, pressing to coat.

*(continued)*

**NUTRITION FACTS:** CALORIES: 494.0 / TOTAL FAT: 15.0 / TRANS FAT: 0.0 / SATURATED FAT: 4.0 / CHOLESTEROL: 88.0 / SODIUM: 654.0 / CARBOHYDRATES: 61.0 / FIBER: 3.0 / SUGAR: 7.0 / PROTEIN: 23.0

5. Place the chicken on the prepared baking sheet and bake for 25 to 30 minutes, until the crust is golden brown and the chicken is completely cooked through and reaches an internal temperature of 165 degrees F.

6. Place the chicken, corn, and cauliflower mashed potatoes into meal prep containers. Refrigerate for up to 3 days. Reheat in the microwave in 30-second intervals until heated through, 2 to 3 minutes total.

## SLOW COOKER CAULIFLOWER MASHED POTATOES

| PREP TIME:<br>20 MINUTES | COOK TIME:<br>6 HOURS | TOTAL TIME:<br>6 HOURS 20 MINUTES | YIELD:<br>8 SERVINGS |
|---|---|---|---|

2 ½ pounds Yukon gold potatoes, peeled and cubed

1 shallot, minced

3 cloves garlic, minced

2 tablespoons unsalted butter

Kosher salt and freshly ground black pepper, to taste

1 head cauliflower, cut into small florets

1 cup vegetable stock

1 (5.2-ounce) package garlic herb cheese, crumbled

½ cup half-and-half

¼ cup chopped fresh chives

This recipe is a favorite from the blog and is so versatile. You won't even taste the cauliflower!

1. Lightly coat the inside of a 4-quart slow cooker with nonstick spray. Place the potatoes, shallot, garlic, and butter in the slow cooker and season with salt and pepper. Without stirring, top with the cauliflower and stock.

2. Cover and cook on low heat for 6 to 7 hours, until tender.

3. Remove the cauliflower mixture from the slow cooker and drain any excess liquid, then return to the pot. Stir in the cheese and half-and-half.

4. Using an electric mixer fitted with the paddle attachment, blend the potatoes and cauliflower until light and fluffy, 2 to 3 minutes. If the mixture is too thick, add more half-and-half as needed. Stir in the chives and season with salt and pepper to taste.

5. Enjoy immediately or add to your meal prep rotation.

# WHITE BEANS WITH SAUSAGE AND STIR-FRIED KALE

| PREP TIME: | COOK TIME: | TOTAL TIME: | YIELD: |
|------------|------------|-------------|--------|
| 20 MINUTES | 30 MINUTES | 50 MINUTES | 6 SERVINGS |

2 tablespoons olive oil, divided

1 (12.8-ounce) package smoked andouille sausage, thinly sliced

1 onion, diced

1 tablespoon chopped fresh rosemary leaves

4 cloves garlic, minced and divided

2 (15.5-ounce) cans cannellini beans, rinsed and drained

1½ cups low-sodium chicken broth

Kosher salt and freshly ground black pepper, to taste

¼ teaspoon crushed red pepper flakes

2 bunches kale, stems removed and leaves chopped

This here is pure comfort food, and it has a few of my favorite things (as Julie Andrews would say): cannellini beans, andouille sausage, and kale.

The consistency and flavor of the cannellini beans really make this dish. Thick and creamy, they are cooked in the browned-up bits of the andouille sausage, which contributes so much really good, salty flavor. The beans are perfectly complemented by garlicky wilted kale, and crushed red pepper flakes provide a little bit of heat. It's simple but you'll be amazed at how this all comes together.

I like to serve this with a Flaky Mile-High Whole Wheat Biscuit (page 205) to soak up all the leftover juices on my plate. We don't want any of this to go to waste! Then, immediately after Butters licks up any biscuit crumbs, we run to the couch to binge on *Friday Night Lights,* because my food stylist, Marian, and I are so obsessed with Tim Riggins right now.

1. Heat 1 tablespoon of the olive oil in a large skillet over medium-high heat. Add the sausage and cook, stirring frequently, until golden brown, 4 to 5 minutes. Transfer to a bowl and set aside.

2. Add the onion to the skillet and cook, stirring often, until translucent, 3 to 4 minutes. Stir in the rosemary and half of the garlic and cook until fragrant, about 1 minute.

3. Stir in the beans and broth. Bring to a boil; reduce the heat and simmer until reduced, about 10 minutes. Using a potato masher, carefully smash the beans until slightly thickened or the desired consistency is reached. Season with salt and pepper to taste.

*(continued)*

**NUTRITION FACTS:** CALORIES: 392.0 / TOTAL FAT: 16.0 / TRANS FAT: 0.0 / SATURATED FAT: 5.0 / CHOLESTEROL: 40.0 / SODIUM: 649.0 / CARBOHYDRATES: 30.0 / FIBER: 17.0 / SUGAR: 1.0 / PROTEIN: 14.0

4. Heat the remaining 1 tablespoon olive oil in a large skillet over medium-high heat. Add the remaining garlic and the red pepper flakes and cook, stirring frequently, until fragrant, about 1 minute. Stir in the kale and cook until wilted, 3 to 4 minutes; season with salt and pepper to taste.

5. Divide the bean mixture and the kale into meal prep containers and top with the sausage. Refrigerate for up to 3 days. Reheat in the microwave in 30-second intervals until heated through.

# THANKSGIVING TV DINNER

| PREP TIME: | COOK TIME: | TOTAL TIME: | YIELD: |
|---|---|---|---|
| 30 MINUTES | 45 MINUTES | 1¼ HOURS | 4 SERVINGS |

### ROASTED TURKEY BREAST

1½ tablespoons unsalted butter, at room temperature

2 cloves garlic, minced

1½ teaspoons chopped fresh thyme

Kosher salt and freshly ground black pepper, to taste

1 (1½-pound) boneless skin-on turkey breast

### GRAVY

1 tablespoon unsalted butter

2 cloves garlic, minced

1 shallot, minced

1½ teaspoons chopped fresh thyme

¼ cup all-purpose flour

2 cups chicken stock

¼ cup dry white wine

Kosher salt and freshly ground black pepper, to taste

¾ pound green beans, trimmed

1 cup Apple-Walnut Sausage Stuffing (page 275)

¼ cup whole berry cranberry sauce

We never celebrated Thanksgiving growing up. I don't know if that was just my household or all Korean households, but we just didn't. So it wasn't until my early 20s that I had my first Thanksgiving meal.

And boy, was I missing out. The turkey, the gravy, the stuffing, the cranberry sauce! No wonder Ross got so mad when someone stole his leftover moist maker sandwich.

But that's beside the point. We now have a complete turkey dinner at our disposal without spending an entire day cooking!

My mission is to have this turkey dinner at least once a week. I have a lot of lost time to make up for!

1. FOR THE TURKEY: Preheat the oven to 375 degrees F. Lightly oil a baking sheet or coat with nonstick spray.

2. Combine the butter, garlic, and thyme; season with salt and pepper. Using your fingers, carefully loosen the skin from the breast meat and spread the butter mixture under the skin. Secure the skin with wooden picks; season the turkey with salt and pepper.

3. Place the turkey on the prepared baking sheet and roast until the turkey is completely cooked through, reaching an internal temperature of 160 degrees F, 40 to 45 minutes. When cool, thinly slice the turkey and divide into 4 portions.

4. FOR THE GRAVY: Melt the butter in a large skillet over medium-high heat. Add the garlic, shallot, and thyme. Cook, stirring occasionally, until tender, 3 to 4 minutes. Whisk in the flour and cook until lightly browned, about 1 minute. Gradually whisk in the stock and wine. Bring to a simmer, stirring occasionally, and cook until the desired consistency is reached, about 5 minutes; season with salt and pepper to taste.

*(continued)*

**NUTRITION FACTS:** CALORIES: 464.0 / TOTAL FAT: 22.0 / TRANS FAT: 0.0 / SATURATED FAT: 10.0 / CHOLESTEROL: 128.0 / SODIUM: 1523.0 / CARBOHYDRATES: 26.0 / FIBER: 1.0 / SUGAR: 8.0 / PROTEIN: 37.0

5. In a large pot of boiling salted water, blanch the green beans until bright green in color, about 2 minutes. Drain well and cool in a bowl of ice water. Drain well and season with salt and pepper to taste.

6. Divide the turkey, gravy, green beans, stuffing, and cranberry sauce into meal prep containers. Will keep covered in the refrigerator 3 to 4 days.  Reheat in the microwave at 30-second intervals until heated through.

# APPLE-WALNUT SAUSAGE STUFFING

| PREP TIME: | COOK TIME: | TOTAL TIME: | YIELD: |
|---|---|---|---|
| 15 MINUTES | 1 HOUR 5 MINUTES | 1 HOUR 20 MINUTES | 8 SERVINGS |

10 cups (1-inch) bread cubes*

1 tablespoon olive oil

1 pound ground mild pork sausage

6 tablespoons unsalted butter

2 cloves garlic, minced

1 onion, diced

1½ cups sliced celery

2 Braeburn apples, cored and chopped

2 tablespoons finely chopped fresh sage

1 tablespoon finely chopped fresh thyme leaves

1 cup toasted walnuts

½ cup finely chopped fresh parsley

Kosher salt and freshly ground black pepper, to taste

2½ cups chicken stock

This favorite from the blog allows you to make ahead a quick and flavorful stuffing that is full of sausage, fresh herbs, and apples.

1. Preheat the oven to 350 degrees F. Lightly oil a 9x13-inch baking dish or coat with nonstick spray.

2. Spread the bread cubes in a single layer on a baking sheet. Bake until crisp and golden, 10 to 12 minutes; set aside.

3. Heat the olive oil in a large skillet over medium heat. Add the sausage and cook until browned, 3 to 5 minutes, making sure to crumble the sausage as it cooks. Transfer the sausage to a bowl and set aside.

4. Melt the butter in the skillet. Add the garlic, onion, and celery and cook, stirring occasionally, until tender, 4 to 5 minutes. Stir in the apples, sage, and thyme and cook until fragrant, about 1 minute.

5. In a large bowl, combine the bread cubes and sausage mixture with the walnuts and parsley; season with salt and pepper. Stir in the stock until absorbed and well combined.

6. Spread the bread mixture into the prepared baking dish. Bake until the top is browned, about 45 minutes.

7. Serve immediately or cool and store in the refrigerator for 3 to 5 days.

**NOTE**
* Can be a mixture of breads such as sourdough, multigrain, whole wheat, or pumpernickel, if desired. Or you can simply use 1 (16-ounce) loaf of your choice.

**NUTRITION FACTS:** CALORIES: 488.0 / TOTAL FAT: 37.0 / TRANS FAT: 0.0 / SATURATED FAT: 11.0 / CHOLESTEROL: 57.0 / SODIUM: 975.0 / CARBOHYDRATES: 36.0 / FIBER: 3.0 / SUGAR: 5.0 / PROTEIN: 13.0

# WHOLE WHEAT PAD THAI BOWLS

| PREP TIME:<br>15 MINUTES | COOK TIME:<br>15 MINUTES | TOTAL TIME:<br>30 MINUTES | YIELD:<br>4 SERVINGS |
|---|---|---|---|

12 ounces whole wheat spaghetti

3 tablespoons reduced-sodium soy sauce

3 tablespoons fresh lime juice

2 tablespoons fish sauce

2 tablespoons light brown sugar

1 tablespoon canola oil

3 cloves garlic, minced

2 green onions, thinly sliced

1 red chile pepper, thinly sliced

2 large eggs, lightly beaten

1½ cups shredded red cabbage

1 large red bell pepper, thinly sliced

1 large carrot, shredded

4 radishes, thinly sliced

½ cup fresh cilantro leaves

¼ cup roasted peanuts

One of our guilty pleasures is ordering chicken pad thai at least once a week. We also pack our order with green curry, chicken sate with extra peanut sauce, and fresh spring rolls with, again, extra peanut sauce.

See, I wasn't kidding. We really pack it in. And after spending $40 for just two people, we said we'd be healthier. And more frugal. So I've been making these whole wheat pad Thai bowls as a compromise, and I have completely fallen in love with them! It's 439 calories per serving and they work perfectly for meal prep!

There's no extra peanut sauce here, unfortunately. But hey, I added plenty more veggies and I swapped in whole wheat spaghetti. Don't get me wrong: I love rice noodles, but they have a very short shelf life. Plus, we save on a few calories here, which just means I make more space for a donut bite for dessert.

Balance, right?

1. In a large pot of boiling salted water, cook the pasta according to package instructions; drain well and set aside.

2. In a small bowl, whisk together the soy sauce, lime juice, fish sauce, and brown sugar; set aside.

3. Heat the canola oil in a large skillet over medium heat. Add the garlic, green onions, and chile. Cook, stirring frequently, until fragrant, about 1 minute. Stir in the eggs and cook, stirring with a rubber spatula, until just cooked through and broken into small pieces, about 30 seconds to 1 minute.

4. Stir in the spaghetti and the soy sauce mixture. Cook, stirring constantly, until the sauce has thickened, 1 to 2 minutes.

5. Serve immediately with the red cabbage, bell pepper, carrot, radishes, cilantro, and peanuts. Or place in meal prep containers and refrigerate for 3 to 4 days. Reheat in the microwave in 30-second intervals until heated through.

**NUTRITION FACTS:** CALORIES: 439.0 / TOTAL FAT: 1.0 / TRANS FAT: 0.0 / SATURATED FAT: 2.0 / CHOLESTEROL: 93.0 / SODIUM: 1095.0 / CARBOHYDRATES: 70.0 / FIBER: 12.0 / SUGAR: 11.0 / PROTEIN: 19.0

# Meal Prep Menu

**NOTES**

| | | |
|---|---|---|
| **MONDAY** | BREAKFAST:<br>LUNCH:<br>DINNER:<br>SNACKS: | |
| **TUESDAY** | BREAKFAST:<br>LUNCH:<br>DINNER:<br>SNACKS: | |
| **WEDNESDAY** | BREAKFAST:<br>LUNCH:<br>DINNER:<br>SNACKS: | |
| **THURSDAY** | BREAKFAST:<br>LUNCH:<br>DINNER:<br>SNACKS: | |
| **FRIDAY** | BREAKFAST:<br>LUNCH:<br>DINNER:<br>SNACKS: | |
| **SATURDAY** | BREAKFAST:<br>LUNCH:<br>DINNER:<br>SNACKS: | |
| **SUNDAY** | BREAKFAST:<br>LUNCH:<br>DINNER:<br>SNACKS: | |

# Meal Prep Shopping List

**PRODUCE**

☐ _____
☐ _____
☐ _____
☐ _____
☐ _____
☐ _____
☐ _____
☐ _____
☐ _____

**MEATS + SEAFOOD**

☐ _____
☐ _____
☐ _____
☐ _____
☐ _____
☐ _____
☐ _____
☐ _____
☐ _____

**DAIRY**

☐ _____
☐ _____
☐ _____
☐ _____
☐ _____
☐ _____
☐ _____
☐ _____

**PANTRY**

☐ _____
☐ _____
☐ _____
☐ _____
☐ _____
☐ _____
☐ _____
☐ _____

**SNACKS**

☐ _____
☐ _____
☐ _____
☐ _____
☐ _____
☐ _____
☐ _____
☐ _____

**MISC.**

☐ _____
☐ _____
☐ _____
☐ _____
☐ _____
☐ _____
☐ _____
☐ _____

# Acknowledgments

To Morgan Hedden, the best "corgi lady" editor on the planet! This is what I called you for the longest time because I couldn't remember your name! Well, actually, I could never remember anyone's names because I'm the worst. So I legit kept referring to you as the "corgi lady." I would tell Maria, "Hey, can we go with corgi lady because she's clearly the best?" In my book, you will always be my favorite corgi lady. Also, you need to get a corgi. Just my two cents.

To Maria Ribas. Can you believe it? Book 2! We did it! Thank you for sticking by my side for this book, and for always having my back, even when I'm frustrated/angry/sad/exhausted—you always seem to make it better. I also can't wait for book 3. I think it's time for a corgi cookbook of some sort, no?

To the entire Grand Central Publishing team, especially Tareth Mitch, Tiffany Sanchez, Linda Duggins, Liz Connor, Karen Murgolo, and Matthew Ballast—thank you for all your hard work!

To my amazing Damn Delicious team—Pam Gibson, Michelle Ferrand, Hristina Misafiris, and Diana Kim—thanks for always putting up with me and making me look like a rock star, even though I'm really just a crazy lady who's obsessed with Butters and all things corgi, donuts, and Dodgers.

To Marian Cooper Cairns. From book 1 to book 2, I feel like we've been through so much these last few years. And all I know is that when I met you during book 1, there was no way I was going to go on in life without you.

Thanks for being so awesome to work with, and for being an amazing, true friend. I will always cherish our donut mornings, our biscuit obsessions, and our Penthouse 5 safe haven where we can talk about anything and everything.

To Jana Nawartschi. I always say this and it's true: I would die without you! I mean, I should probably say this to Ben but really, thank you so much for making my life a hundred thousand times easier, for always taking care of Butters, bringing donuts and Starbucks to shoot days, and always accepting all of my meltdown emails in the wee hours of the morning.

To Butters, thank you for being the crumb police, for drooling on my computer when I'm working, and for being so mischievous during the most stressful work hours. Mama still loves your poo-eating face.

To Ben, my future 2020 husband, thank you for always being there. For being so patient with me and for taste-testing everything and saying it's amazing because you love me (even though sometimes it wasn't very good). In reality, that makes you the worst taste tester, but still, I love you. (To Pluto.)

Finally, thank you to all of the *Damn Delicious* readers! Without you, this book would not have been possible. Thank you for following along, especially when I'm rambling on about Butters, and for making a dream a reality. Now excuse me while I go cry my eyes out. I love you all!

# Index

## C

# About the Author

**Chungah Rhee** is the writer, recipe developer, and photographer behind the incredibly popular blog *Damn Delicious*. She has a bachelor's degree from the University of California, Los Angeles, and a master's degree in public health from the University of Southern California.

Started in 2011 as a hobby, *Damn Delicious* has since grown to become a full-time job and business. Chungah and her recipes are regularly featured in major media such as *People, Better Homes & Gardens, Bon Appétit*, the Cooking Channel, HGTV, *Redbook, The Kitchn, Huffington Post*, and *Buzzfeed*, among others. Her first book, *Damn Delicious: 100 Super Easy, Super Fast Recipes*, was published in 2016 by Oxmoor House.

Today, she cooks nonstop alongside her favorite assistant, Butters, the Insta-famous corgi (you can find him hamming it up @butterscorgigram). Chungah, Butters, and her soon-to-be husband, Ben, all live, play, and eat in Los Angeles.

ALSO BY **CHUNGAH RHEE**

*Damn Delicious:*
*100 Super Easy, Super Fast Recipes*